HOW I TEACH FOCUSING

D1222814

HOW
I TEACH
FOCUSING

Discovering the Gift of Your Inner Wisdom

BEBE SIMON

with Rosa Zubizarreta

to Mary Elaine,
with all best wishes,
Rosa Zubizarreta

Mill City Press,
Minneapolis

Copyright © 2014 by Bebe Simon

Mill City Press, Inc.
322 First Avenue N, 5th floor
Minneapolis, MN 55401
612.455.2293
www.millcitypublishing.com

All rights reserved. No part of this publication may be reproduced, stored in a retrieval system, or transmitted, in any form or by any means, electronic, mechanical, photocopying, recording, or otherwise, without the prior written permission of the author.

Text copyright by Bebe Simon and Rosa Zubizarreta.
Articles reprinted by permission.

ISBN-13: 978-1-63413-115-5
LCCN: 2014920129

Cover photo by Cheryl Luft
Cover Design by B. Cook
Typeset by Sophie Chi

Printed in the United States of America

Dedicated to Eugene Gendlin and Mary McGuire

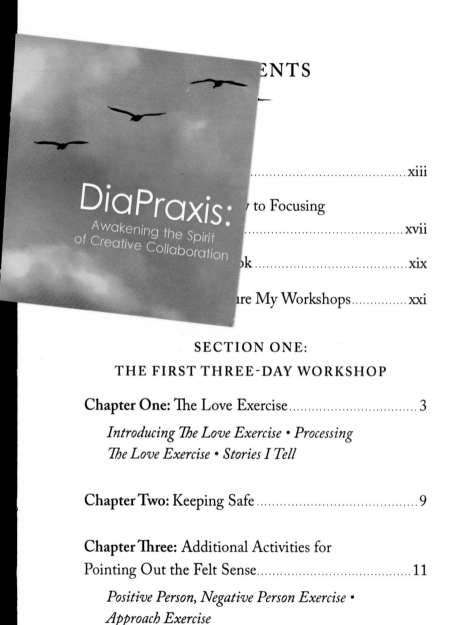

CO**NTS**

....xiii

to Focusing

....xvii

ok...xix

re My Workshops..............xxi

SECTION ONE:
THE FIRST THREE-DAY WORKSHOP

Chapter One: The Love Exercise...................................3

*Introducing The Love Exercise • Processing
The Love Exercise • Stories I Tell*

Chapter Two: Keeping Safe...9

Chapter Three: Additional Activities for
Pointing Out the Felt Sense.......................................11

*Positive Person, Negative Person Exercise •
Approach Exercise*

Chapter Four: Moving into Listening............15

Round Robin • "Focuser as Teacher" •
Homework for Day One

Chapter Five: Beginning Day Two..............19

Coaching Support for Listeners • Demonstrating
"Bad Listening" • On "Not Asking Questions"

Chapter Six: Deepening Our Practice...........23

Choosing Who Will Go First in a Pair •
Choosing a Topic • More on "Coaching the Listener" •
Reflecting What We <u>See</u> as Well as What We <u>Hear</u>

Chapter Seven: Preparing students for
working independently..............29

A guided Focusing experience for each person •
The phone exercise • More on 'Choosing a Focusing topic' •
"Homework" Between the Two Workshops

SECTION TWO:
THE SECOND THREE-DAY WORKSHOP

Chapter Eight: Encouraging Participation.........35

Opening with an Attunement • Starting
Again with Listening

Chapter Nine: How I Teach Guiding..........39

The Focusing Attitude • Awareness of Language •
Trusting the Focuser's Process • Developing One's
Own Style in Guiding • Practicing Guiding

Chapter Ten: Working Together with
Other Teachers 45

Individual Variations in Teaching Styles

Chapter Eleven: How I Teach Interactive
Focusing 49

Chapter Twelve: The Decision-Making Exercise 55

SECTION THREE:

MORE ON HELPING PEOPLE LEARN FOCUSING

Chapter Thirteen: Working with Potential
Challenges 61

*Learning a New Language • When People Have a
Hard Time Accessing the Felt Sense • Giving People
Permission to "Not Tell the Story"*

Chapter Fourteen: Advanced Workshops,
Changes Groups, and Alumni groups 67

*My Pattern for a Changes Group • Working
with New People in a Changes Group • Advanced
Practice Group*

SECTION FOUR:

BEBE SIMON'S COLLECTED WRITINGS

Overview by Rosa Zubizarreta 73

Articles Published in the Focusing Connection

Can you take those inside and see what
they would be like in your body?....................79

Focusing on the Good 81

More on the Critic and Other Parental Voices........85

Giving the Ending A Chance............................89

What if You are Stuck?.................................91

Just Saying Hello.....................................93

Listening to Your Inner Place of Wisdom...............95

After Hello: The Bridge to Right Relationship........99

Focusing Recollections: The first "Hello"
and More..103

The Power of Helloby Ann Weiser Cornell...........107

Articles Published Elsewhere

Focusing for Life.....................................113

"It needs to make sense".............................119

A Meeting Placeby Rob Foxcroft.......................143

Previously Unpublished Articles

Another View of "Yes, But"...........................153

A Method of Focusing for Self-Empathy
in Stressful Situations...............................155

Bebe the Storyteller, with Focusing Tales
of Wonderment..161

Bebe's Thoughts on Guiding (brief version)...........171

Bebe's Thoughts on Guiding (longer version)........175

Acknowledgments 187

Postcript..188

FOREWORD

I FIRST MET BEBE SIMON IN 2004, at the International Focusing Conference in Costa Rica. I had been studying and practicing Focusing since 1998, and this was the first time I had been able to attend the International conference. Reviewing the rich and varied menu of offerings, I found myself drawn to the workshop that Bebe was leading, with the simple and direct title of "How I Teach Focusing."

Since I had studied Focusing with a few different teachers by then, I was surprised to discover the strong impact that Bebe's fresh approach to teaching had on me. I remember approaching her after the workshop, and asking her whether she had a book that contained what she had taught us. That initial encounter was the seed of what you are now holding in your hand.

At the time, Bebe was already one of the honored elders in our community. She originally began teaching Focusing in 1980 as one of the people who assisted Eugene Gendlin in his workshops. After Gene and the Focusing Institute moved from Chicago to New York, Bebe continued teaching Focusing workshops in the Chicago area, where she has lived since 1951. Every year, she unfailingly travels to wherever the

International Focusing Conference is being held, to learn, to teach, to share her inimitable stories, and to reconnect with friends both old and new.

Due to family and other life circumstances, my own participation in the International gatherings has been much less constant. It was not until the conference in California in 2011 that Bebe and I met again and picked up the thread where we had left off in Costa Rica. She had not forgotten my enthusiasm for her work, nor the idea of creating a book together about her unique approach to Focusing.

That fall, we began a series of phone interviews that I wrote up and sent to her for her review. Bebe's commitment to being her own authentic self extends to her relationship to technology. While she still works three days a week in a medical office where computers abound, she has chosen to not have a computer at home and continues to communicate via telephone and letters instead of e-mail. So we have needed to create a collaborative writing process suited to our unique circumstances; I was able to negotiate the use of a fax machine to send her drafts, which she would review assiduously and note the desired changes in order to communicate these back to me during our next phone call.

While Bebe's tastes in technology might be regarded as somewhat conservative, her signature approach to Focusing practice, remains not only classic and timeless but also fresh and relevant. For instance, with all of the recent developments in positive psychology, many of us are beginning to realize that Focusing is not only useful for healing from trauma, but is also a powerful way to nourish ourselves more fully by deepening our positive experiences and unfolding their rich intricacy.

Yet this is not news to Bebe. While many new Focus days are unfamiliar with Gene's original "Love e........., Bebe's intuition about the power of the positive has led her to continue using this exercise as the foundation for how she begins a Focusing workshop. Bebe greatly enjoys sharing this exercise at Focusing International conferences with people who have never heard of it before.

Another example: In Bebe's experiential workshop in Costa Rica, she led us through several of the initial exercises that she uses when teaching Focusing. In the process, I was surprised to encounter her "How to keep yourself safe" exercise, as I had taken Focusing workshops with several other teachers, and never encountered this key exercise before.

Several years later, I was at a meeting where Focusing-Oriented Psychotherapists were discussing their concerns about how the careless use of Focusing might inadvertently overwhelm certain clients by leading them into closer contact with traumatic memories that might prove too much for them to handle. While Focusing is in general a very safe practice, I believe that the safety exercise that Bebe always includes in her workshops is one way to make it even safer, by explicitly teaching Focusers that they are the ones who need to set the boundaries on their own inner explorations.

As Focusing has been spreading in the underdeveloped world[1], we are learning about creative new approaches to teaching Focusing that these gifted Focusing teachers have

---

1   I am thinking especially of Nina Joy Lawrence and Patricia Omidian's work in Afghanistan and Pakistan, as well as William Hernandez' work in Ecuador.

developed to adapt to different circumstances and conditions. Instead of the more typical approach of offering four "levels" of Focusing taught in four separate weekends over the course of a one or two-year period, we are now seeing much more experimentation in both format and teaching methods.

As you will see in the following pages, Bebe Simon has been creating her own new formats and teaching methods for quite some time now, and freely sharing them with those who have been fortunate enough to attend her yearly offerings at the Focusing International. The intention of this book is to share her work more widely with others in the larger Focusing community. May it serve as an inspiration for your own on-going exploration, of the unique way in which *you* can share Focusing practice with others.

Rosa Zubizarreta
November 4, 2012

A SPECIAL NOTE FOR THOSE
NEW TO FOCUSING

WELCOME! SINCE WE'VE written this book primarily for those who have already had some exposure to Focusing, I could easily use that as an excuse for not even attempting to answer the difficult question of, "What is Focusing?" There are many different ways one might respond to this question, but since this is a book by and about Bebe, I'll quote her and say that "Focusing is a way of learning how to be guided by our own inner wisdom."

When we are Focusing, we learn to pay attention to something called the "felt sense." This term, now in widespread use in our culture, was originally coined by Eugene Gendlin. The founder of Focusing, Gendlin was the research director for Carl Rogers. While Focusing itself may not have a high profile, it has influenced many forms of body-based therapy, including Hakomi and Somatic Experiencing. It has also influenced many spiritual teachers and forms of spiritual healing, from Buddhist psychologist Tara Brach to beloved Jewish renewal teacher Rabbi Zalman Schechter-Shalomi, of blessed memory.

Focusing is a practice for just about everyone. It is true that many psychologists and counselors study Focusing to learn how to listen better to their own clients, and also to learn how to listen better to their own inner process. Yet some of the best Focusers in the world are regular, ordinary people, with *no* special training in psychology or counseling. Instead, they might be artists, or writers, or mechanics, or hairdressers, who have gained years of experience with the "listening inside" practice we call Focusing. Since Focusing is often done in partnership pairs, this means that they also have years of experience with offering supportive listening to their Focusing partners.

OK. That's it for now. Instead of saying any more about Focusing here, I would rather invite you to read this book, enjoy the detailed descriptions of how Bebe teaches her workshops, and imagine what it might be like to be a participant. Afterward, if you are interested in learning more, you can visit the Focusing Institute's website at www.focusing.org to find a teacher near you.

Unless of course, you are lucky enough to live in the Chicago area where Bebe Simon is still offering her Focusing workshops. You can visit Bebe's website at www.FocusingForLife.org, and then phone her at 708-524-1114 for more information or for a free session.

Rosa Zubizarreta

HOW TO USE THIS BOOK

MY INTENTION WITH THIS BOOK is to inspire others to find their own way of teaching Focusing.

The process of learning Focusing is very individual. Sometimes a particular thing happens that is very interesting, but that does not happen very often. I have included several examples of that kind in this book, just to show how individual the process can be, and to help people realize that this kind of thing *can* happen.

At the same time, it's important to not expect that something similar will happen when you teach Focusing. And we should certainly *not* be trying to make something unusual happen; that would be a mistake. I do want to encourage you to pay attention, and to notice whatever unusual things may occur as you teach; they may be quite different than the ones I have written about here.

I also want to say that my teaching has evolved over time. Some of the things I write about here, I have done for a long time. Others I have just started doing in the last few years, as I am continually getting new ideas and learning from others. So if you have taken a workshop with me in the past, you might be surprised to find some things in here that are new. And you may want to consider coming back for another workshop. Even if much of the material is the same, it is always a new experience.

I often use a lot of stories when I teach. The stories tend to change, depending on the situation, and so it's hard to show that aspect of my work. I do want to encourage people who are teaching Focusing to share your own stories. When something comes to you, something that you have experienced in some way, it's often good to share it with the people you are teaching.

HOW I STRUCTURE
MY WORKSHOPS

FOR MANY YEARS, I ASSISTED Gene Gendlin with his monthly weekend workshops. Later on, after the Focusing Institute had created a four-level system for teaching workshops, I was asked to take over the teaching of the Level One and Level Two workshops. However, when I started teaching Focusing on my own, I decided that levels was not the best approach. What happened is that sometimes people would take the first level, and then two years later, come back and want to take the second level. And in the meantime, they might not have been using Focusing at all in the interim.

The way I teach now is by offering a 6-day training. We begin with a three-day workshop, that is followed a month later with another three-day workshop. This gives people time to practice what they have learned, and to come back with questions. So now I offer everything that was included before in Levels 1-4, in these two three-day workshops, with a month in between for people to practice.

In the first three days, the emphasis is on teaching listening. We start by using round-robins. Then we have people working in pairs, and we go around and help each person tening, if they don't know how to reflect back to the speaker. *[Note to the reader: all of this will be described in greater detail in the pages that follow.]*

We also emphasize the idea of "Focuser as Teacher" – how you as the person who is taking a Focusing/speaking turn, can help your partner become a good listener for you, by asking for a reflection, saying what doesn't feel right, asking to hear the reflection again.

Between the two workshops, people practice with a partner. They are asked to practice at least one hour a week, but if they want to do more, that's up to them. The partners are just listening to each other, not guiding.

Guiding is something that doesn't come until the second workshop. During the first workshop, they experience what it is like to be guided, since we make a point of giving them individual time with a trainer, so that they can experience their own Focusing process. So they experience being guided, but they are not taught how to Guide.

In addition to Guiding, during the second workshop I teach Interactive Focusing, the importance of language, and the differences between what we do in Focusing Partnership, and the usual things that we do socially -- in other words, the things you would ordinarily do in your life, but that we don't do here, for good reason.

For example, here in Focusing, we want you to ask for what you want, and to take responsibility for taking care of yourself. This is not an easy thing for most people, as we are taught to be kind and thoughtful, and take care of everyone else. Also, here in Focusing, we don't ask questions of the person who is taking a Focusing turn, and we don't offer them suggestions for how to "fix" a problem. While I introduce this in the first workshop, it is important to review it in the second workshop, also.

After people have taken the two workshops, they are welcome to continue in two ways. One is in the free Changes group that meets weekly at my house, and has been doing so for the last 25 years. The other is through an advanced practice group of my students that meets monthly. I will be describing both of these groups in more detail in a later section.

SECTION ONE:

THE FIRST THREE-DAY
WORKSHOP

1

THE LOVE EXERCISE

GENE GENDLIN IS THE ONE who originally created the
Love exercise. He used to start every workshop with it. What
Gene would do is to start with the Love exercise, even before
asking people to share their names! He would just start right
in with it, as the very first thing.

What I do is begin by inviting people to say their names,
what brought them here, and what they already know about
Focusing, if anything. I also like to let people know, how to
be comfortable in this space: how they can get something
to drink, where the bathroom is, etc. Then, we start with the
Love exercise.

Introducing the Love Exercise

The first thing I do is tell people that Focusing is *not* just about
problem-solving. Instead, we can make good things even
better, by using this approach. And so I guide them through
the Love Exercise.

"Start by thinking about something that you love… not a person, and not a pet. It could be an object, a place, or an activity. But for the purpose of this exercise, choose one thing. It doesn't have to be the thing that you love the most. Just choose whatever comes to your mind first…"

"The next step is, think about one or two reasons why you love this.

This part here is thinking – you are not yet Focusing, just thinking about it."

Now, so I can try to keep up with the rhythm of the whole group, I ask them to

please raise a finger when they have something. That way I know when they are ready to go on.

"Now go inside, and imagine that you are being with the thing you picked. You might be looking at it, using it, feeling it, or doing it… whatever is appropriate, depending on what kind of thing it might be…

Notice how it feels, when you are with it. Find some words to describe to yourself, how it feels… and then check and see if that's the right description. See if the place inside says "yes" to that description…

Now I am going to offer a question. This question is not for you to answer, not something to figure out. Just ask this inside, with wonder and curiosity. You may need to ask more than once, and then just wait… wait… for something new to come, something different than what you said earlier, about why you loved this.

The question to ask inside is, 'What about the thing I picked, makes this ___ feeling?'

And you can use the description you found earlier. Here's an example:

'What about this thing makes this warm fuzzy inside?'

And if something comes to you, notice how it feels,

when it comes to you.
Is it different than why you said you loved it, earlier?
Something unexpected?"

Processing the Love Exercise

Once I lead the group through the Love Exercise, the next thing I do is ask for anyone who may have gotten stuck, who would like some help. It's good for everyone in the room to see that I can help with a problem when they are stuck.

I also invite them to notice, if they are stuck: How does it feel to be stuck? Because that's a felt sense, too. At the same time, I remind them again that this exercise is NOT a test, and there is no way that they can be doing it "wrong."

One way to help might be to have them go over each step from the start of the exercise, and talk about what happened during that step, to see how far they got and where they had gotten stuck.

Or I might ask, "How far did you get, before you got stuck?" That way I would see where they need help.

Sometimes it might be that they didn't understand something that I asked them to do, and didn't feel free to ask for a clarification. I always tell people to feel free at any point to ask a question or make a comment. I don't mind being interrupted. And this holds true for ALL of the exercises that we do. Still, people don't always feel comfortable asking questions, especially at first.

Often, someone may have gotten stuck at the point where I said that the question to take inside is not a question to answer to me, or even to themselves, but rather something to ask and wait, and to maybe even ask more than once. And that's not ning that is easy for people to catch on to. So if that is where they got stuck I start at that point,.

I invite them to go slow, to ask the question and wait, to just be curious and to wonder. To ask the question inside themselves, and then wait for something new to come – something different from what they said in the first place, about why they chose that particular thing – something that they didn't expect, or wouldn't have thought to say.

This is what I do with *any* exercise: if they are stuck, I invite them to re-do where they got stuck, help them to slow down, and hopefully *not* have them feel that there is something wrong with them, because they didn't get it.

If no one asks for help, then I go on to ask who would like to share, whatever happened in that particular exercise. This sequence, of first inviting anyone who got stuck and would like some help, then asking for people's experiences, applies to all of the exercises I do.

Stories I Tell

When I am teaching the Love Exercise, I often like to tell the following story about a time when a person who knew Focusing quite well was with us. I don't quite remember why she was with us, but she was with us as we were doing the Love Exercise.

This person chose something that she was very fond of doing, and it was needlework. She knew that the reason she loved it was because of the beautiful things she made. Then, as she did the exercise, and connected with how she felt inside while she was doing needlework, she realized that it was also peaceful, and that was why she loved it. She had not been aware of *that* before.

A short time later, I was teaching again. It happened that this same person was with us, for the second time in a brief while. I was leading the Love exercise again. Fortunately, she did not ask me if it was OK to pick the same thing, because if she had, I probably would have said, "Oh, why don't you pick something else." At the time, I didn't know any different, and so that's what I probably would have said.

But she didn't ask, which was good, and she ended up picking up the same thing. And this time, she knew at the start of the exercise that the reason she loved the needlework, was both because it was beautiful and peaceful. Yet now, as she looked deeper, as she imagined herself doing needlework and connected with how she felt inside, she discovered something new: she discovered that when doing needlework, she was "sewing herself together."

When this person shared what she had found with the group afterward, everyone in the room felt chills as she said it, we were so taken with it. I also learned from this that there are always deeper levels that we can go to, even if we are looking at the same thing. This is my favorite story about the Love Exercise, and I always tell it when I am teaching.

Another short anecdote related to the Love Exercise is a very powerful incident that has only happened once.

I was doing a demonstration with a large group. The people in the group came from many countries, and were involved in a variety of religious orders. One of the men in the room had a very distinctive appearance. He was wearing a black t-shirt that had something to do with motorcycles, and looked a bit tough with a pencil behind his ear. At some point I learned that he worked with young people on the street, which gave me more context to understand the initial impact he had on me.

When we were about to start the Love exercise, this person asked whether he could pick an activity, and I said yes of course, he could pick anything. Then, when we had completed the exercise and were ready to share, this man responded immediately and was very anxious to share. He raised his hand, jumped up when I called on him, and then, in that moment, as he was about to tell us what he had found earlier during the exercise ,he suddenly had a new realization.

This man discovered that it was the *love*, not the *thing*, which made the feeling! He had not realized this until the instant he was going to share, and then he knew. It was a wonderful moment. He was deeply moved by this, as were we all.

2

KEEPING SAFE

ONE OF THE NEXT THINGS I do, right after the Love Exercise, is to show people how to keep themselves safe during the workshop. I explain to them that I can't keep them safe, but that *they* can. And then I show them how, with this two-part exercise:

> *"Think of something that makes you uncomfortable. This can be something that has happened, or something that might happen, that you know would make you feel uncomfortable.*
>
> *Notice how it feels as you imagine that thing. What would be the right description, for that feeling?*
>
> *Now check inside, to see if that is the right description… if something inside agrees, that this is how you felt, or would feel.*
>
> *Now set that aside for a little bit, and go on to the second part.*
>
> *Think of something that has made, or would make you feel, unsafe.*

ple, if you are driving and someone almost
ff, think of how frightening that is, even if you
10 get hit.

So, it doesn't have to be something that really happened,
but the fright is still real, and you know that this is unsafe."

Now notice, what is the description of THAT
feeling (pause), and check inside, to see if that's the right
description.

Next, we talk about both of these inner feelings:

"Being **uncomfortable**, can be very good for Focusing,
because when you pay attention to it, you can learn more
about what that is, and why it affects you in that way.

But **unsafe** says NO, don't go there. And when you
have that feeling, you need to listen to it. That's how you
can keep yourself safe, by paying attention to it when it
says NO.

Eventually, with good listening, you might also be able
to look at that place that feels unsafe, without having to go
there, maybe from quite a distance away. The unsafe thing
might be in one place, and you might be across the room, or
across the street, or across the river. But when you are just
beginning, it's important to notice that 'no,' and stop, even
if its something in an exercise that a Focusing teacher is
leading."

This is how I teach people how to keep themselves safe
when using Focusing. I feel it's an important thing, and
something we should always include when teaching Focusing.

3

ADDITIONAL ACTIVITIES FOR POINTING OUT THE "FELT SENSE"

AFTER THESE FIRST TWO exercises, I make time to point out to people what we have been doing:

"As you have been doing the Love Exercise, and the Keeping Safe Exercise, we have also been giving you an opportunity to get in touch with what we call the felt sense., and 'the inside place.'"

Not everyone may get it right away, but this will give many people some idea of what a felt sense is. We then continue with other exercises, not always in the same order. The purpose of all of these exercises is to offer more opportunities to learn about the felt sense by becoming acquainted with it, and by experiencing what their body can offer them.

Positive Person and Negative Person Exercise

This exercise demonstrates the felt sense by noticing how you would feel in two different situations.

"First, imagine someone you can't stand... someone that you wouldn't want to waste your time talking to. It doesn't have to be anyone you actually know; it could be someone in public life, a political figure. You just know that you wouldn't be interested in having a conversation with this person. Let me know when you have thought of someone like that. If you have, please raise a finger." (This helps me keep up with the group...)

Now, I'm going to tell you that this person has just walked into the room, especially to see you, to spend time with you. How does that feel? Is there a word or phrase to describe that feeling? Do you have the description? Now just set that aside for a minute.

For the next half of the exercise, think of someone you would love to spend time with, but it just can't happen. It's not possible – maybe the person has already passed on, or there is some other reason that it just can't happen. Again, let me know when you have thought of someone like that. If you have, please raise a finger.

Now I'm going to tell you that this person has just walked into the room, especially to see you, and to spend time with you. Now, how does that feel? And what would describe that feeling accurately, so that the inside place would say 'Yes, that's it. That's the right description.' It could be a word, a phrase, or an image.

If anyone is stuck, or wants help with this, that's fine, let me know. Also, feel free to let me know if you need me to repeat a question, if it's not clear. It's ok to let me know right away."

If anyone is stuck, we would go over the exercise step by step, to see where they had bumped into something, or skipped something. Sometimes something else jumps in. I can help them slow the process down, do it at their speed, and point out what the next piece might be. Meanwhile, the rest of the group is learning from observing as I am working with an individual person.

After everyone has completed the exercise, I will ask, "Does anyone want to share what they got? What that exercise was like for you?" They can share either part, it doesn't matter. Then I point out to them that even though they know that this isn't really happening, "Your body gives you the feelings, as if it were real – and *that* is the felt sense."

Usually some people will share the person they chose, and what came to them. Sometimes people are deeply touched by this exercise. Again, the purpose of it is to illustrate the felt sense, including what their body can experience in response to a person or thing, even when it isn't really happening.

The Approach Exercise

I first demonstrate this exercise to the whole group, and then ask people to break into pairs, and go off into other rooms to do it themselves.

In the demonstration there are two of us, standing about 8 feet apart. One of us is the first to approach. The other is the person who is waiting. That person's role is to signal "Close enough / no more" by raising their hand when they sense the need to stop the person who is approaching from coming any further.

When the person who is waiting gives the signal to stop,

the person who was approaching stops and then backs up just a few steps. This lets the person who is waiting see if that feels better, to be a little further apart.

Then the person who is approaching comes forward again to the distance that felt "too close," so the other person can experience that again. They repeat this a few times, backing up to the "just enough" distance... pausing so the other person can feel that, and then coming forward again.

Before sending people off in pairs, I let them know that both people will be getting a turn. Once the person who is waiting has had the opportunity to experience how the different distances feel, the two people will switch. The one who was approaching before is now the one who'll wait, while the one who was waiting before will now approach.

I also ask them to wait before they talk about their experience with the exercise. After each person has had a turn, then they can talk about it, but not until then. Afterward, they can talk about how it was for each of them.

4

MOVING INTO LISTENING

THE LOVE EXERCISE, the Safety Exercise, the Positive-Negative Person Exercise, and the Approach Exercise, are the first exercises we do at the beginning of the workshop. With each one, there is room to stop if someone wants help, if they got stuck, or if they wish to share. However many people want to share their experience is fine. After people share, if I have a story, that's when I tell it.

I also encourage people to be comfortable, to help themselves to whatever they need: a glass of water, an extra pillow. I remind them that they are free to do things and ask for things as they need them. I also tell them that sometimes I forget about taking a break, and am glad when people remind me. I welcome them to help me design the workshop as we go along.

After all of these exercises, it is probably time for a supper break. I usually bring in a pizza, so that they don't have to go out. On the first day, Friday, we usually go from 2pm to 8 pm,

only have to take off a few hours from work in the
.hen Saturday and Sunday are both from 10:30 am

After supper on the first day, we might be ready to start with the listening. We move into it slowly, with a round-robin at first. We usually continue with the listening on the second day. This kind of listening is helpful in two ways. Listening is what we do when we accompany a person who is Focusing. It's also how we relate to our inside places when we ourselves are Focusing.

Listening Round-Robin

We begin to learn listening with a round robin. The group is in a circle, and we start with one person listening to the person who is sitting next to them. For the next turn, the person who was listening becomes the speaker, and the person on their other side becomes the next listener. In this way, we go around the circle.

At first, we ask the speakers to say just one sentence, so that the listener has something very short to reflect. That's how we start. And then we gradually go around the circle again, with each person having 3-5 minutes. I ask the speakers to pause frequently during their turn, to give the listeners an opportunity to reflect. If the speaker doesn't stop, it is much harder for a beginner to be able to interrupt them so that they can reflect back what they are hearing.

However, it's often difficult for speakers to remember to pause to receive a listening reflection. Thus, I also encourage the listeners to become more assertive in this regard. I tell them that I know how difficult it can be to interrupt someone.

Yet at the same time, as a listener, we are not h
speaker by letting them go on and on. If we do, \
going to be able to remember what they said, and w~~~~ ~~ be
able to reflect it. Even though in the rest of the world it may
seem rude to interrupt, here it is important that we are able to
stop a person, so that we can offer them a reflection.

"Focuser as Teacher"

Another thing I teach my students as part of learning to listen,
is the key role of what I refer to as "Focuser as Teacher." I tell
them that you aren't likely to get a good listener, unless you are
willing to help teach others how to listen to you. For example,
you need to become comfortable making requests such as "I
need you to say that back to me," or, "Could you say that back
to me again?" For many people, this is very different than what
they are used to in interacting with others. It can feel very
difficult to ask someone to give them a reflection, if that person
has just been sitting there listening to them.

As part of learning to listen, we sometimes ask the speaker
to offer feedback to the listener such as what was most helpful,
and what didn't feel so good.

Homework for Day One

At the end of the first day, we might give people some
homework. As part of the workshop, we give people a manual
that includes some articles. The manual also includes lots of
blank pages for notes, so that they can make it a personal
journal of their own experiences. After each exercise, I
encourage people to write something down about what came
for them, what that exercise was like for them.

For homework, I may ask them to read an article from the manual about listening, and also to review whatever notes they may have made during that day.

5

—⁓—

BEGINNING DAY TWO

ON THE MORNING of the second and third days I like to start with an attunement. I guide the students for a few minutes, inviting them to notice how it feels inside, to be in the room, now that they already know some people here. I invite them to notice whether there is anything that they may want to say, that is left over from the day before – a question they may want to ask, or anything they would like to ask for, that would help them be more comfortable here. I tell them that you can't promise the inside place that it will get what it wants, but you *can* promise that you will ask for what it wants.

I also invite the students to see if there is anything inside from the reading, or from how it felt on their way here today. I suggest that they say hello to the inside place, using their own name: "Hello, x, how are you feeling today? What would you like to have happen today? Is there anything that didn't feel good from yesterday, that you want me to tell her (the teacher)?"

After I finish leading the attunement, I invite them to share anything that came for them, any questions, requests, etc. I remind them that the more people that speak up, the better the workshop will be, as it will help me respond to their needs.

Coaching Support for Listeners

Next we continue with the listening, in pairs or small groups. Each group will have a teacher with them. First though, we introduce the idea that the teacher is there as a coach, and we talk about what coaching means. The coach is there to support the listener. Sometimes a listener may be thinking about two different responses they might offer to the person who is speaking, and is not sure which way to go, so they may want to ask for help. If they don't ask for help, we won't usually step in unless we feel that there is something that the listener didn't hear. In that case, the coach will step in to help them even if they haven't asked for help.

When we invite people to break into smaller groups so they can take longer turns, the teachers stay in each room, and are available to coach the listeners if they get stuck and don't know what to say. We've worked out a system of a hand signal for this. If the teacher sees that things aren't going well, we can use a hand-signal to call "time out." Then we offer the listener a suggestion of what they might say, what might be a more effective response at this point.

A Demo on "Bad Listening"

One of the things I used to do in my workshops was to demonstrate what "bad listening" looked like. I would listen to my assistant, who would take a speaking turn in front of the room. As a listener, I would do all the "wrong things", and it amused people because it was so obvious. I would jump in, and tell my assistant what he should be feeling, all those ridiculous things that are so very common in our society.

Even though my assistant knew me so well, and knew I would never hurt him, he would still reach a point during the demonstration where he couldn't stand it any more, and would have to stop me. Then we would do a retake and start over, on the same topic that he had originally chosen. But this time, I would listen in the way that we want people to listen in our Focusing work. And the participants could see very clearly the difference between the two different ways of listening.

I don't do this kind of demonstration any more, because I no longer have that particular teaching assistant. However, the point of the demonstration was to make a strong impression about how we listen in a Focusing context. We do not ask questions, we do not try to fix things – all of the things that happen so often in society, that lead people to feel that they have not been listened to. We don't do that here in the workshop. Our goal is, we want to hear people the way they need to be heard.

On "Not Asking Questions"

Of course, when I am teaching, it is fine for people to ask me questions if they don't understand something. What I am talking about here is not asking questions when someone is Focusing and we are listening to them.

The reason for that is, when we ask a question, we are leading someone in a certain direction. And that may not be the direction that their inside place needed to go. Many people find it difficult to say "no" to what someone else is saying to them. Often they end up in the position of taking care of the listener, rather than following their own path. So that's why we don't want the listener to be asking questions. Here, we want people to have the freedom to take what they need, and only accept what feels right.

Another distinction is that when we guide people through a Focusing session, sometimes we offer them questions that they can take inside. Yet at this point we are not talking about guiding, we are talking about just listening. It's important to make a clear distinction between listening, which is a basic foundation practice, and guiding, which is a more advanced skill. Sometimes people try to guide not because the situation calls for it, but because they don't know how to do simple listening. Very often, basic listening is all that is really needed. We stress the importance early on of learning to listen well, as basic listening will be used throughout the rest of the workshop.

6

———

DEEPENING OUR PRACTICE

ON DAY TWO, I continue to work with students on how we listen to our Focusing Partners, and also continue to point out opportunities to listen to our inside places.

Choosing Who Will Go First in a Pair

Whenever students are working in pairs, and we ask them who wants to go first, they tend to look at the other person. This is an opportunity to invite them to learn to pay attention *inside*. Here is how I do this. I start by inviting the students to say inside, "I'm going to go first," and see how that feels. Do they sense something inside that says, "YES!"? Or is there something inside saying, "No, no, not yet...." Or else they can say inside, "I'm *not* going to go first." And then notice, "Is something inside relieved? Or is it disappointed instead?"

I have the students play this little game of saying one thing or the other to the inside place, and then listening to notice how the place responds. I tell the students that if it turns out that both people are wanting to go first, that's *my* problem as a teacher. They don't need to take care of each other, or to take care of me. They only need to find out, if their inside place would be happy to go first, or not.

This becomes another way of learning to listen to the felt sense. I use every opportunity I can to get them used to listening to their inner wisdom!

What is most common is for them to discover that neither of them wants to go first, rather than that both of them wants to go first. When that happens, I have to go by my sense of the people, and of what would be best, and use my own judgment. It's easier if it works out that each of them gets their first choice, but it doesn't always happen that way!

Choosing a Topic

With regard to the person who is speaking, there are two ways to start the process. We begin by asking a yes or no question such as, "Do you have something you want to work on?" If not, then we suggest that the speaker asks inside, "How am I, right now?" I also explain to them that what is going on in the workshop right now is as legitimate to work on as anything else. They don't need to come up with a particular problem. It could be that they got up that day, and didn't feel like coming. They don't have to have a specific thing to work with. Whatever happened that day, either outside or inside the workshop, can be a legitimate thing to work on.

More on Coaching the Listener

When a listener gives a time-out signal to pause their listening practice and get some coaching help from us, the listener is the one who needs to ask their partner, the Focuser, to pause. Then the listener communicates with their coach. Once the listener has gotten the answer to their question, he or she is the one who needs to give that reflection back to the Focuser, so they can reconnect.

Of course the Focuser has been present throughout the consultation between the listener and the coach, so it's quite likely that they have already heard the suggestion. But it is different when it is coming from their listener. I don't want them to switch to having me be their listener. Instead, as the listener offers something back to the Focuser, it helps the two of them to reconnect. So we try to keep the flow going between the listener and the Focuser, even though there is a coach there. Along the same lines, whenever the Focuser corrects the listener, it's very important for the listener to say the new statement back to the Focuser, in the corrected way. This is another aspect of keeping the flow going between the listener and the Focuser.

Sometimes it may be the coach who is calling for the time-out, because she notices something. It might be that the Focuser is working on something very difficult, beyond the skill of the listener. In those situations, I may end up interacting with the Focuser directly. If I am the one asking for a time out, then I may take the processing a step or two further along, by offering suggestions directly to the Focuser. But then afterward, I still need to find a way to reconnect the listener and the Focuser. Sometimes, after I have helped the Focuser take a step or two, I may signal the listener with my hand: "OK, you go back to them now, it's time for you to take over again."

Sometimes, when we are learning how to listen to the Focuser and reflect back their words, some students may be concerned about reflecting and see it as "just parroting back" another person's words. I respond by telling them that this is just the way that we begin, and that afterward, we will be exploring other levels of reflection. Yet even when we are more advanced, basic reflection can still be helpful. Whenever we don't know what to say, it is usually safe to use the Focuser's own words.

At the same time, even when we reflect back to someone *exactly* what they have said, the Focuser might still say no, that's not quite right. This could be because as they hear it back, they realize, that isn't what they *needed* to say. Often when the speaker says, "No, it's actually more like…" they are connecting to something that is more fitting to what they want to be getting across. So the correction is about their own discovery process; it is *not* a judgment of the listener as a person. What we are doing when we reflect is not about being perfect. Instead, it's about allowing the person to be heard, in the way they need to be heard, so they have the possibility of going deeper into their own experience.

Reflecting What We See as Well as What We Hear

Another thing I teach people is to reflect not only what they hear, but also what they see. For instance, if I see something, I might say, "Oh, there's a smile there…." or, "There's a tear that comes, right there in that place. Something was touched…." Sometimes, the Focuser may not be aware of it. It may go by so quickly, that if you didn't say it, they wouldn't realize that's what had happened.

Sometimes there is an expression on the face that changes, so I know that somebody was touched inside by being listened to, or by being offered a reflection. I might do some guiding at that point: "Be very gentle there, something was touched...." They will often nod their head in response, and I will reflect back, "Ah, there is a yes there...." I will encourage the person who is speaking to take their time, and be gentle with the place that was touched.

7

PREPARING STUDENTS FOR
INDEPENDENT PRACTICE

ONE OF THE AIMS of the first workshop is to prepare students to practice on their own, in the month before the second workshop. Students will be practicing in pairs, taking turns being the Focuser, the person who is listening to their inside place, and speaking from that, and being the listener, the person who is listening to the Focuser and reflecting back whatever he or she says.

A Guided Focusing Experience for Each Person

On Saturday and Sunday, one thing we try to do each day is to give each person an opportunity to have a turn with one of the trainers so that we can guide them, and they get to have a sense of what their own Focusing process can be like.

Usually when we are guiding a student, there is also a third person, another student, who is observing. We tell the student who is observing that it is OK to watch the person who is

Focusing, so that they can tell what it is I am responding to as a guide. This is not what people are used to; in this culture, it is not considered polite to look. Yet if you don't look, you'll miss the cues that lead me to say what I say when I am guiding. So I encourage them to watch, because often that is not easy for people to do.

After they have watched me guiding, the person who is observing can then ask me anything they want. I remind them that we never ask anything of the person who just had their process, since they may need to stay with their inner experience for a while longer. Of course that person is there hearing what we are saying, and can jump in if they want. It is just that we don't deliberately ask them anything, since it could take them away from what they may need to be with at that moment.

The Phone Exercise

This is an exercise we do to prepare students for their phone appointments with each other after the workshop. I have them pair up by twos, and sit back to back, either in chairs or on the floor. They are sitting back to back so that they can't actually see each other. Then I ask them to imagine that they are holding a phone to their ear, and to take five minute turns listening to each other.

I want to demonstrate that you can do this work without seeing the other person. We always do this exercise before the end of the first workshop, as some people are not comfortable at first with the idea of doing Focusing over the phone. Of course we don't want to force people to do anything. We want to encourage them to only do what feels right to them. However, the exercise is an opportunity to help them become more comfortable with Focusing over the phone.

And, we remind them that even though it's only a five-minute turn each way, it still has to be something real that you care about, otherwise Focusing won't work. It has to be something real for you.

This reminds me of a little story that Pete and Ed tell. They usually take Focusing turns every morning. One morning, one of them had burned the toast. Then he found that even though he tried, he couldn't focus on anything else, until he got what the burned toast was all about. It was something very real for him. Even though somebody else might say, "Oh, that's nothing, that's not a big thing, it's nothing to worry about," to *him*, it was very real, to the point where it kept him from Focusing on anything else, until he had spent some time with it. It was just *there*, and he couldn't let it go.

More on "Choosing a Focusing Topic"

When we are first doing listening practice, I ask the people who are Focusing to not pick anything big. I do want them to pick something that is *real*, but not something that is a major problem. People don't always understand this very easily. Once after giving these instructions, a person started their Focusing turn by saying, "I just started to get a divorce!"

I understand how if something is "up" for someone, they might have a hard time *not* talking about it. At the same time, if it is something that big, it can be a difficult thing for someone new to listen to. And, it can also be a difficult thing for the speaker to talk about briefly.

So I remind people that they don't have to keep coming up with "problems" as a topic for when it's their turn to

Focus. Rather, they could Focus on how they feel about how the workshop is going, or how they felt about the trip in this morning. Maybe they wanted to stay in bed! I want them to choose something *real*, but not major, so that they can handle it a bit more easily.

"Homework" Between the Two Workshops

After the first workshop, I encourage students to read a little ahead in the manual before next time. I encourage them to read about guiding, which is what we will be teaching next. And I also encourage them to partner with each other, and to practice taking turns "just listening" while their partner is Focusing.

SECTION TWO:

THE SECOND THREE-DAY WORKSHOP

8

ENCOURAGING PARTICIPATION

BY THE TIME WE HAVE gotten to this stage of the learning process, I want participants to be helping to design the workshop based on what their needs are. Still, some people don't seem to have so much to say, while others are ready to jump in; some are more comfortable speaking in groups, others less so. Yet the more people say, the more I can respond to whatever their needs are. So what is on my mind as I begin the second workshop is encouraging their participation.

Opening with an Attunement
As participants are returning to a place and a group with which they are already familiar, we usually start with an attunement. We invite participants to get a body sense of how it feels to be here right now. We ask, "As you sense inside, are there any things that come to you that you would like to report, or comment or ask questions about?" There isn't always something, but if there is, I want to make an opening for people to speak.

This is also an opportunity to encourage them to be open, and remind them that they do not need to find a problem to talk about. Anything can be material to talk about. We can use anything that is happening right now as material to process, or it might be something about what happened when they woke up, or were getting ready to come here this morning.

In addition to sensing how it is right now, I invite people to talk about how it has been for them during this month in which they have supposedly been practicing with each other. I don't assume either way, whether they have or not; some people may have had the opportunity to practice, others may not. Some people may have been busy, and others are not so comfortable doing Focusing on the phone. In any case, I like to leave it open, for whatever their experience has been. Then, in response to what participants share, I will often share a story or an anecdote.

Starting Again with Listening

Next, I may do another exercise with them. If we have not had time during the first workshop to do the Decision-Making Exercise, I may want to do that. Otherwise, I may lead them in another round of the Love Exercise to get them started again. Only this time, instead of reporting out to the group as a whole and having me listen to them, I want them to work with each other afterwards. I will invite them to form pairs or small groups to listen to each other about what they experienced in the exercise.

The purpose here is to have them begin with another experience of *listening*, before we move into learning about guiding. The general principle is to have them see what the results of just listening might be before deciding whether guiding may be required or useful.

Some people prefer guiding, because it gives them something to do. So they will jump into guiding, without having paid attention to whether this situation is one where listening alone is adequate and guiding is not really needed. So before teaching guiding, I want to encourage people to pay attention to whether it is really needed or not.

9

<hr>

HOW I TEACH GUIDING

WHEN WE START TALKING about guiding, I usually ask students to turn to the page in the manual where I have written about this: "Bebe's Thoughts on Guiding."

I explain to the participants that the title is deliberate. These are only *my* thoughts on guiding; there are other ways of guiding as well. I might also tell the story of how I came to write this piece.

Many years ago, someone who was part of our early work in Focusing was moving to Iowa. She was very sad to be moving, and so we all agreed that if she wanted us to come and offer a workshop there, we would do so. Sure enough, she ended up organizing something through the university there, and about half a dozen of us came out to give a Focusing workshop.

Once we were there, someone asked me if I would

> say something about guiding. I had not prepared this
> beforehand, but I was willing to do so. I gathered
> together some thoughts, and gave an impromptu
> presentation. People really liked it, and afterward they
> asked me for copies of my notes. And that's how this
> piece came to be written.

Next we talk about each of the points in "Bebe's Thoughts about Guiding."

The Focusing Attitude.

For me, "being with" is the phrase that captures the essence of the "Focusing Attitude", that is, the attitude we attempt to hold while Focusing. Other people talk about it in different ways. Yet for me, "being with" someone whenever we are listening to them or guiding them, is primary. What does it take to really *be with* someone? That, to me, is the Focusing Attitude.

Awareness of Language

Being aware of language includes awareness of both the language that we ourselves are using, as well s the language that the person who we are listening to is using. Ann Weiser Cornell has helped us have a big awareness of this.

One point in this regard is to be aware of what we call fire-engine words. If you are sitting in a room and traffic is going by outside, you won't always hear the traffic, but you will always hear a fire-engine going by. Some words are like that; they stand out through the emphasis the person is giving them.

We *always* want to reflect the fire-engine words.

Another thing to keep in mind, is that whenever we don't know what to reflect as a listener, it is generally safe to use a person's own words.

Trusting the Focuser's Process

Even when we are offering guiding suggestions, we need to trust the Focuser's process to be the ultimate guide and to set limits. Only IT, that is, the Focuser's inner place, knows what it needs. And so any guiding we do needs to be offered only as a suggestion, not as a command. This means "yes" or "no" must be equally welcome responses to any suggestion we offer.

It means that whenever a suggestion does *not* fit, and the Focuser lets us know that, our role is to go back to listening and reflecting. In this case, it's often helpful to go back and reflect the last thing the Focuser said, before we offered a suggestion.

Developing One's Own Style in Guiding

I like to remind people that we will each end up finding our own style of guiding that feels right to us, and that becomes our own. At first, it's natural to copy other people's forms of guiding. Eventually, though, we will find our own style.

At the same time, some people only enjoy listening, and they will not want to guide. And nothing I say seems to change that! Some people will only use the simplest form of guiding, such as, "If it feels right, go inside and be with that." They do not seem comfortable suggesting things, nor coming up with original ideas of their own. They are very good listeners, and don't seem to need to go beyond that. We cannot require or force anyone to start guiding; it's there if they wish to learn it, but it is not something that everyone is comfortable with.

I do suggest to people that their reticence to use guiding could be a good thing to Focus on. While they are taking some time to listen inside, they might want to ask themselves, "What's in the way of my being comfortable with guiding?" And some people may not want to explore what's there. As teachers, we must make room for whatever a person is going to do, and not make them feel that they are failing, just because they are not doing something we might suggest.

Practicing Guiding

After we have gone over what guiding is, we have people work in pairs, with one of us present as a coach. We are there primarily to support the listener/guide, rather than the Focuser.

At the same time, before starting out we remind everyone that the Focuser is the teacher. What we mean by this is that the best way to get what one needs when Focusing is to teach the listener by giving them feedback on what more (or less) is needed, what we want them to reflect back or to repeat.

Once the pairs have started taking their Focusing/ Listening turns, we are available as coaches if the person who is listening/guiding would like some help. We might also call a time out and offer some help, if we see that the listener hasn't heard something that the Focuser said. In that kind of situation we might interrupt, and offer some possible ways that the listener might be responding.

Some people may pick up on a suggestion quickly, others not at all. When I am stepping in, I usually explain why it seems important to me to attend to some particular thing that the Focuser has said.

After we have gone over the page on guiding, and practiced it in small groups, I let people know that their homework that evening will be to look through the manual, at all of the materials on guiding, and also at any notes that they have taken during the workshop about their experiences in guiding or in being guided.

10

WORKING TOGETHER WITH
OTHER TEACHERS

JUST AS WE DID IN THE FIRST workshop, in the second
workshop we also want to give each person an opportunity
to be guided by each of the teachers. We want them to get a
chance to know what their own process is like, and what feels
good for them. This is one of the reasons I like to have small
workshops, and to work with assistant teachers so we can have
a low teacher-student ratio.

However, sometimes these few sessions of being guided
by each teacher, are not enough for someone to really become
comfortable with their own inner process. Sometimes it may
take more than a few sessions for a person to get a sense of
what the experience of Focusing is like, for them – to learn
what their own process feels like and what it requires, and what
they like or don't like about how we are guiding them. In those
situations, if the person is interested, we find other ways of
continuing to work with them.

Individual Variations in Teaching Styles

One of the things that happens with teaching another teacher is that we each have our own style of teaching. When we are working in small groups, I'm not in the room with the other teacher, and so I can't respond to what they are doing. They may be doing something very different than what I do. This too is valuable, as it helps give students a sense that each person has their own style.

Part of my style is to use different situations as opportunities to invite people to sense into whatever else might be happening. So if someone says they are feeling too tired to do an exercise, I would say to them, "Tired of... question mark?" And then I add, "Don't try to figure it out, just wonder and be curious and see if something new wants to come..." Very often, that will bring something new and interesting for that person. It becomes an opportunity to look at what the process can do, rather than just assuming that if they are tired, it is time to rest.

Or, for example, if someone says they are frustrated, I might invite them to explore, "Frustrated about... question mark?" Whenever I have a question for them to use, I invite people to take the question inside, to *not* answer it right away, but instead to just wait and see if something comes, something that they wouldn't have thought of otherwise...

Other kinds of questions like this include "What is the best of it?" whenever someone is describing something happy, or "What is the worst of it?" whenever someone is describing something difficult. The invitation is to *not* answer the question, to *not* try to figure it out, but to just ask…and wonder… and be curious… and wait… and see what might come.

This is something I do a lot of, whenever it seems that it might be appropriate or useful.

11

HOW I TEACH
INTERACTIVE FOCUSING

WHEN I AM TEACHING, I also teach Interactive Focusing. I can usually do this in a fairly short amount of time, with someone who already knows Focusing. Sometimes I teach this as part of the second workshop.

Interactive Focusing can be done between two people, or it can be done as a whole group. The process begins with someone who wants to be listened to. There is no guiding, just reflecting back what the person is saying. That is one difference from regular Focusing.

The person who is speaking will speak for three to five minutes, until they feel that they have said whatever they need to say about that topic. We call that a "piece." Sometimes with a newer person, the listener may need to ask, "Does that feel like a piece?" Or if the person is more experienced, they may say, "Ok, I'm complete for now, that feels like a piece."

The next part is the empathic moment. This is something

that is not part of regular Focusing. Both people – both the speaker *and* the listener – go inside, to see if they can get an image, a word, or a phrase that captures the heart or the core of what they have just heard. It's not about repeating the story at this point.

This is much more difficult for the speaker to do for themselves, especially when they are just learning. So what I often suggest is for them to imagine that they have been listening to someone *else* speaking... say, an interview on TV. That often helps the speaker to get enough of a distance from their own content, so that they can get a sense of what is the core of what they have just said.

Both the listener and the speaker wait until they *both* have something. Then when they do, they signal to each other, or say, "Yes, I have something."The listener then asks the speaker, "Do you want me to go first, or would you like to go first?" It is the speaker's choice who will go first, but they each get a turn.

When the listener offers their empathic moment, the speaker does not need to take care of the listener. That is, if the speaker doesn't want to, they don't have to say anything about the empathic moment they have just received. If in fact they are touched by it, they can choose to take another minute or two to take it in. Or, if they want to, they can choose to give feedback about how the empathic moment affected them – but they don't have to.

So each person, both the listener and the speaker, takes a turn saying what they received when they sensed inside for an empathic moment. Once that is complete, we switch. If we are working in pairs, the listener now becomes the speaker, and the speaker becomes the listener.

Now the second person is free to pick up on something that the first person said – something that somehow connects for them, in their own life. It doesn't have to be the same thing as what the first speaker was talking about; it can be very dissimilar. The point is just that it connects somehow, to some portion of what the first speaker shared. And this is another way in which Interactive Focusing is different from regular Focusing.

The second speaker now says their piece, and then the two of them do the empathic moment, in the same way we have just described above.

We have developed a slightly different format for working with Interactive Focusing in groups. If the rest of the group were to just sit there while two people are doing Interactive Focusing, they could easily become tired or bored. What we have found is that when the empathic moment comes up, it's possible for everyone to participate. Each person in the group can then take a turn, offering to the listener what they received when they went inside to sense for an empathic moment. This makes participating in the group very alive for everyone. Of course, if someone is not the primary listener, they can always choose to pass – they don't have to offer something to the speaker as an empathic moment.

Also, when we are doing Interactive Focusing in a group, the speaker and the listener don't exchange roles at the end of a turn. The person who was listening before gets to be the new speaker, but the person who was speaking gets to rest for a while. The new listener is the person sitting on the other side of the new speaker, who was an observer before. And that's how we go around the circle.

This has worked well for us, as a way of keeping the whole group together and involved. It also serves to help people find connections among one another. Each person who takes a turn picks up on something from what the person before them has said. This, plus the addition of the empathic moments is what makes the process interactive.

Interactive Focusing can be very gratifying and quite amazing at times. I remember once a woman was speaking in one of the groups. At the end of her turn, when the person who was listening went inside, what came to him during the empathic moment was the image of a dollhouse. When he offered this to the woman, she was very moved. She said, "Oh my goodness, when I was 10 years old I had a dollhouse that I used to play with all the time. I have not thought about it since then!" This woman had not said anything about the dollhouse during her turn, only after the listener offered his empathic moment.

Very often what people receive in the empathic moment is an image. Even people who don't usually get images, or expect to, will often be surprised at what comes up.

When people are describing what they got when they went inside, it's important to remind them to not explain or apologize for it. People have a tendency to say, "Well, this is crazy, this doesn't really fit…" Well, it *does* fit. Just say it… don't apologize for it!

The person who was speaking is the one who will decide what is useful to them or not.

Interactive Focusing can also be adapted to work when two people are having an interpersonal conflict. I remember working with a couple who had some conflict. Sometimes it is difficult to reflect something back when it is a personal issue between you. In those kinds of situations, you would need a third person to sit with you, so that the third person can pick up and be the listener for a moment.

12

THE DECISION-MAKING EXERCISE

I FIRST LEARNED THIS EXERCISE at a conference in Germany, and I have taken it home and used it often. This is the way it works:

I tell people to think about something that they need to make a decision about. For example, "Should I call her, or shouldn't I?" "Should I go, or shouldn't I go?"

Then I ask them to choose, without telling me, which is A and which is B from their two choices. I have them do this, without their knowing ahead of time what I will do next.

Next I tell them that they don't need to think about their problem any more, because the decision has already been made for them. They are going to do "B". (I'm assuming people usually will pick "A" as their first choice, so I purposely say "B".) Very often this startles them a bit. I say, "OK, how did that feel inside?"

Then I say, "OK, put that aside for a minute. Now, the decision has already been made for you, you don't need to think about it anymore. Now, you are going to do 'A'."

Now I ask them how *that* feels. If both choices feel about the same, then I invite the person to spend some time going back and forth between how each choice feels, and notice whether a third choice presents itself. It usually does!

Then I often tell them the story of how I learned this process, and what my own experience with it had been.

I was attending the International Focusing conference, and I had made arrangements to visit a friend after the conference. It was going to be in the middle of the week, and I began to be concerned that it might not be very convenient for my friend to have me stay with her on a work night. I had started to worry ,"What if I get there, and feel like I shouldn't have come?" I didn't want to be imposing on her, and I was worried that since I didn't have a car, I wouldn't be able to just turn around and leave.

Someone had already agreed to take me to this friend's house after the conference. The next day I would be going back on a train, to the place where I was staying. So if it turned out that either my friend or I was feeling uncomfortable, I would be stuck, and I would have to stay over anyway until the next day.

So the decision I had to make was, "do I go, or not go?" I did not want to miss seeing my friend, so not going didn't feel good. Yet to go and feel that I shouldn't have didn't feel good either. Either way, it didn't feel good.

So as I was doing the exercise, and going back and forth between how each of the options felt, a third option just popped in – call her up and ask her! Find out ahead of time, if it would be inconvenient or not. I had not even considered that option before.

And so I did call, and my friend assured me that she wanted me to come. I took my ride out there, we went out to dinner, and we had a lovely time together. And when my friend had to go to work the next morning, she had already arranged for her daughter to take me to the train. I was feeling very satisfied with how it had all turned out, and it showed me the importance of checking out decisions ahead of time.

So what I offer people is the possibility of waiting to see if there is a third choice that might be much better than the two that they have been considering.

I have another story I tell that is also about how Focusing can help with decision-making.

I was with a friend who knew Focusing well. She asked me to listen to her about the choices that she had between two different work opportunities. After having spent years preparing for this career, she now had to choose between these two possibilities.

My friend wanted me to help her, as her decision was not easy. And so she told me about one opportunity which had some things she liked very much, but also some things that didn't feel quite right. It was a similar situation with the other opportunity: There were some things she liked about that one, and also something that didn't feel quite right.

I happened to know this friend well enough; she had a husband who was employed, and was not desperate for work in order to survive. And so I said to her, "What if you decided to not take *either* of these opportunities at this time?" And she very quickly said, "Oh, no! Then I wouldn't have *anything* to hang on to!"

Now I knew that it might be helpful for her to Focus on something else first, rather than just on the decision. So I said to her, "Oh, there's someplace here that needs something to hang on to…" She had not been aware of that before, so I suggested she spend some time with that place, and see what the "needing something to hang on to" was all about.

This made sense to her. After she took time to do that, she felt relieved, and was able to make her own decision about the jobs.

MORE ON HELPING PEOPLE LEARN FOCUSING

13

WORKING WITH POTENTIAL CHALLENGES

Learning a New Language

Sometimes when people have something else that they already know how to do, there is a risk that they will end up doing that instead, and won't learn Focusing. I explain this to people with an example. Say you are very comfortable in a particular language (for instance, Spanish) and, you are also starting to learn French. Of course, the language you are comfortable in already is much easier for you to use. But if you want to learn the new language, you need to stop using the other one for a while. You need to first set aside what is easier and more comfortable, and then afterward, you can explore the connections between the two, find the commonalities.

Focusing is a new language, and for the time being, students will need to set aside what is more familiar in order to learn a new language. I always explain this, but it doesn't always work! It can be hard to get people to set aside what they are familiar with. It's a very good thing for them to know, whatever this other practice of theirs is, but it often does get in the way of learning a new language.

One recent example of this was a gentleman who was having difficulty learning Focusing. I didn't realize what the difficulty was, until something he said helped me realize that he was doing what he always did in therapy, and this was getting in the way of his learning to Focus. When I realized this, I told him that he needed to let go of doing what he always did for now, and do something different in here with me.

When People Have a Hard Time Accessing a Felt Sense

Sometimes some people have a particularly hard time accessing a felt sense. It can be frustrating for them when that happens. Yet if and when they finally do access it, the experience can be particularly rewarding.

I remember a time when someone who was a PhD in psychology wanted to learn Focusing from me. At that time, my teaching format consisted of four 2-day workshops. This gentleman didn't seem to feel anything and yet things would come to him when he did the exercises. He could find "next steps" that would seem to be forward moving, but he did not seem to be aware of a felt sense. Finally, on the last weekend, he finally got what the felt sense was, and realized that he hadn't gotten this before.

Up to that point, he was getting something from the workshop that was valuable to him, something that was keeping him interested and coming back. He lived quite far away, so this was a significant effort for him. He had gotten steps forward, even though these steps did not seem to be attached to a felt sense. But now he had finally gotten what a felt sense was. He had gotten it from the inside, from feeling it himself, and he was delighted.

When people are having a hard time connecting with a felt sense, what I do tends to depend on the situation. It's very individual. Sometimes I will work on the phone with someone, in between the first weekend and the second one. Or, I might suggest that they might work with a partner. I also offer a two-day advanced workshop, and I host a monthly meeting for people who have taken the basic workshop with me. People can use any of these formats as opportunities to keep learning.

When I'm working with someone who is having a hard time accessing a felt sense, I try not to make a big deal about it, so that people don't get obsessed with it. I don't ask them, "Where in your body are you feeling that?" because that's just frustrating to someone when they can't access a felt sense. Instead, I just focus on helping them be a good listener to their "inside place".

Giving People Permission to Not Tell the Story

Listening well to someone can be a very powerful experience. When I'm listening to someone Focus, I'm clear that I don't need to hear the content of what they are processing. I start by asking people, "Do you have something already there, that you want to work on? You can just let me know, yes or no…" Some people *want* to say what that something is -- that's ok, it's their choice – but it's important for me to let them know that they don't *have* to say it.

Even if someone wants to share what it is, it's often much better to not say it right away. I sometimes say to people, "Let me know when you have something. But don't tell me what it is– first, have it for yourself. Then ask – ask it, if it is ok to tell: 'Should I tell her?' And then listen, listen to what it says…"

Even if you are generally an open person, not guarded, what is inside might not want you to talk about it. And so it's always good to check, first. So when people tell me, "I have something," then I ask them to notice, "How did it feel, when that something came?" And then they can see if it is ok to tell me. I don't have any problem if they want to tell me, I just want to make sure, that it is right for them.

Sometimes it works very well, to invite people to do Focusing without telling me the story. Other times, people know that they do need to tell their story. It needs to be their choice. I tell them, "I don't know what you need. Only your inside place does. You don't have to say anything that you are not comfortable saying – and if you *do* say something, it's for you, not for me. I don't need it."

I show students how to Focus and listen in this way during the first workshop, by demonstrating what it's like to talk about something without saying what it is about. I give them an example, such as: "Every time this person does that, I get so annoyed…" When I say this, I, as the Focuser know what I am talking about… yet the listener doesn't know who the person is, what my relationship is to that person, nor even what it is that this person did that got me so upset. And they don't need to know any of this to be a good listener for me.

Not having to share details has been a very big experience for some people, as it creates enormous safety to not have to talk about what they are being with, inside.

I have had a few particular experiences that show the power of this approach. One was with a man that I did not know at all at the time. Yet some of the other participants had recommended to him that he work with me during the guided session in the workshop. This was near the end of the workshop, when each of the participants could pick someone to work with, for a half hour.

So he asked to work with me, and I said yes. When he started his turn, he said in a weary way, "Well, I guess I have to tell the story all over again if I want help." And I responded, "Absolutely not! *You* know the story... you don't need to tell it to me. Can you just think about how the story feels, inside? And then, can you be with that place, that is feeling that?"

The man was silent for a long time, and then he gasped, "It's on my side! I thought it was the enemy!"

I've never forgotten that experience, how his insight literally took his breath away. We ended up becoming best friends, but I never asked him what it was that had happened in his process. It doesn't matter to me – I can enjoy what happens with the process, without needing to know the content of the problem.

14

ADVANCED WORKSHOPS, CHANGES GROUPS, AND PRACTICE GROUPS

IN ADDITION TO THE BASIC six-day training, I also sometimes teach an advanced workshop. This is a two-day workshop in which I include some dreamwork and more about guiding, the critic, and whatever each person in the group wants more of. I also enjoy leading a Changes group, which I will describe here in more detail.

My Pattern for a Changes Group

In addition to teaching workshops, I have also been leading a Changes group for 25 years now. There is no charge for it, and anyone can come. We have it at my home every single week, once a week, on Tuesday nights.

To create the format for the group, I asked myself, "What could I do, that I could continue to do over time, without feeling any pressure?" And that's how I designed the group.

I teach people how to make themselves comfortable in my house, so I don't have to serve as hostess. That way I can make it comfortable for me to keep having the group. No snacks or drinks are provided.

It used to be that I had a very dear friend who would take the key whenever I was out of town, so that this group ran, whether I was there or not! She has since passed away, but there is another person who will take the keys, so the group can continue to meet. When I am out of town, they will come and open the house, and wait 20 minutes or so, to see if anyone shows up.

You see, I have a policy that you do not need to let me know that you are coming. This way, you can just come when it feels right to come. Before, sometimes people would call, and then they would not come. So it's easier to just have it be a drop-in group. And however many people show up, is exactly the right number!

If someone doesn't know anything about Focusing and wants to learn, they can come two times to just observe. And if they want to, they can be listened to, without being expected to listen to anyone. After that, if they want to continue coming to the Changes group, they can choose to take a Focusing course somewhere; – it doesn't have to be from me.

We start each evening at 7:45 p.m. If there is anyone new, then someone will start by explaining the house rules: where the closet is to hang up your coat, where the bathroom is, how to help yourself and get a drink of water if you need one.

Then we begin with "news and goods,", as a way of saying hello. It's an opportunity to share something, if you want to share. No one ever has to say anything – they can just say,

"I pass." And if "news and goods" doesn't fit, you can share something "recent and meaningful."

Next people ask for what they would like, and we break up into groups of twos or threes. People go into different rooms to take their focusing turns. This part generally lasts about an hour, from 8:15 p.m.to 9:15 p.m..

Lastly, we come back together as a group, to share any "news and goods" from our time together this evening. These are generally very recent and meaningful! Again, it is not necessary to share, and not everyone does. When people do, it's generally brief – they don't go into the details of their focusing session, just a short highlight. And then we end at 9:30 p.m., with a form of good-bye – hugs, handshakes, or whatever is comfortable.

Working with New People in a Changes Group

Whenever we have a new person in a Changes group, I always take them with me when we break up into pairs or small groups. I usually will have another person there with me as well, so the new person can observe how we listen to each other.

So for the first turn, I will listen as the other person takes a Focusing turn. The new person is invited to observe. After that turn ends, I will invite the new person to ask any questions that they want of me as a listener – but not of the person who has just finished Focusing.

That person is still there, and they can hear us talking, and may jump in if they want to say something. But I am clear with the new person that we are not asking the Focuser any questions, that we are just leaving them be in case they still need to be with whatever they have just processed.

For the next turn, I will let the new person know that they can have a turn if they want one. If they don't, if they just want to continue observing, that's fine too. That's their option.

If they do want a turn, then usually I will be the one who will listen to them. And I will likely do more guiding than I would otherwise. Afterward, I would probably mention that to them, too: that after we have learned Focusing, we don't usually need much guiding from the other person, but that when someone is new, we might do a little more of it at first.

Advanced Practice Group

In addition to the Changes group, I also host a once-a-month group that meets on Sunday afternoons for three hours. This group is only for people who have taken my course. Each person pays a small fee to attend, and I provide snacks.

Someone from the group volunteers to lead that day. First, they suggest that everyone take a few minutes to go inside, and see what they would like to share – something recent that has happened in their lives. If a new person is present, we each say our names before sharing.

Next, the leader suggests that we again go inside, and see what we would like to have for the afternoon. Partner focusing, or interactive focusing with the whole group? Or, there may be something that they want from me – to teach something, or to do an individual session. I am there to be available for whatever the group asks of me.

This group has been going for fifteen years. I enjoy it very much, and participants also enjoy it.

SECTION FOUR:

BEBE'S COLLECTED WRITINGS

BRIEF OVERVIEW

BY ROSA ZUBIZARRETA

IT HAS BEEN AN HONOR and a pleasure, to bring together all the various articles that Bebe has written over the years. It was also a bit daunting initially, since very few of these writings were in electronic form. I am very grateful to Ann Weiser Cornell for putting out a call for volunteers in her 19th Day Gazette, and deeply thankful to all of the people who responded to that call. Many volunteers contributed by transcribing one or more of these articles from a photocopied, typed, or even handwritten page to an electronic format. This honor roll includes: Ina Bransome (*Can you take those inside...*), Mary Elaine Kiener (*Another View of Yes* and *Focusing on the Good*), Lyn Rosen (*More on the Inner Critic*), Carol J. Sutherland Nickerson (*What if You are Stuck* and *Giving the Ending a Chance*), Leonard Grossman (*After Hello*), Adrianne Nevon (*Listening to Your Inner Place of Wisdom*), Chiara Gelardin (*Just Saying Hello*), Joke Van Hoeck (*Bebe, the Storyteller, with Focusing Tales of Wonderment*), Jim Leonidas (*Focusing for Life*), and Jane Nelson (*Focusing in Stressful Situations*). Our deep thanks to each of you, for helping to make this compilation possible!

I also want to mention a few things about the articles you will find in the following pages. I have placed them in three basic groups: first, all of the articles that Bebe wrote for *The Focusing Connection*, the delightful newsletter that Ann Weiser Cornell created in 1984. Bebe wrote an article for the inaugural issue, and continued to contribute articles over the years. The only article in this group that is not by Bebe is an article by Ann Weiser Cornell, acknowledging how Bebe influenced her own approach to Focusing.

The second group includes two articles published elsewhere: an article by Bebe published in *The Monthly Aspectarian*, and an in-depth interview of Bebe by Rob Foxcroft. A later version of this interview was published in the Focusing Folio. It offers a behind-the-scenes view not only of Bebe herself, but also of Gene Gendlin, Mary McGuire, and other elders in our Focusing community. Also included in this section is a poem that Rob Foxcroft wrote to Bebe as a birthday gift, and that captures so well the particular sensibility that Bebe brings to Focusing.

The third section, last but not least, is a series of articles that (to my knowledge) have not been previously published. These include an article on a particular "crossing" between Focusing and NVC. This is one of the earliest pieces of writing on a subject that has become more popular over the years, and is another example of how Bebe has always been so far ahead of her time. This section also includes the transcript of a "true Focusing stories" session that Bebe offered at a Focusing International Conference in 1991. And, in closing, we have included two different versions of "Bebe's Thoughts on Guiding."

Why two versions, you might ask? Well, in her papers Bebe found two versions that she had started at two different times. While in each case the first few paragraphs are somewhat similar, each essay then diverges in its own unique direction. I asked Bebe which of the two versions she preferred; she responded that she liked each of them for different reasons. I supposed we might have attempted to combine them both into a single document. Yet, given that this is one of the key areas in which Bebe has contributed so much, I thought it might be helpful to keep both versions – thus offering a glimpse into the many different ways in which Bebe can expound upon this central theme.

This may be a good place to acknowledge a larger point, about a certain degree of repetition that is in this book. Bebe uses certain stories from a lifetime of practice to illuminate teaching points in her workshops, as well as in her writings. If you were to read this book from cover to cover, you would likely find a few stories that show up more than once, though they may not always be told in exactly the same way. For better and worse, we have chosen to let this stand. Getting to know this book might be a bit like getting to know a person; it's likely you might end up hearing a particular story more than once, yet the richness and texture of a deepening relationship transcend mere repetition.

So here it is: a compilation of Bebe's writings to date, full of relevant insights that are still fresh, as well as inspiring stories that offer us a window into the larger world of Focusing. Enjoy!

ARTICLES PUBLISHED
IN THE
FOCUSING CONNECTION

CAN YOU TAKE THOSE INSIDE AND SEE WHAT THEY WOULD BE LIKE IN YOUR BODY?

*originally published in the first issue of The
Focusing Connection, March 1984*

THIS IS A TIME WHEN I AM working with a person who knows Focusing, a coordinator from another city. He expresses interest in seeing how I work and asks me to treat him as I would anyone else. I ask if he would like to start with clearing a space and he says yes. Just as we get started with "see how you are inside", "acknowledge what comes" and "find a comfortable way to place it outside for now", he tells me that when he sits down he has a problem of falling asleep, and that at that moment he is recognizing the symptoms – tingling of the face and heavy eyes that want to close. I think a moment and suggest a Focusing move that often works with physical sensations – I ask if he can take those physical things inside and see what they would be like in his body. He is startled by my suggestion – obviously, that's one he hasn't heard before. I repeat the words, "Can you see how they would feel if they were inside?"

So he sits quietly for a minute or so (not long), and then

says, "Relaxing." I'm not sure where he is in the process. Did he get a felt sense and is that the quality? In other words, did the handle come right with the body sense? I ask him this, and he says, "No, I don't think so." I'm stopped for a moment, as he repeats that it would feel relaxing. He seems very satisfied with that and is breathing deeply but easily.

Then I get a flash and ask if he is saying he got the answer before the question. He grabs that so quickly there is no doubt we are on the same wavelength. He says. "Yes!" Yes! That's it!" and I know we have finished a whole step. I have thoughts about what happened but I save them for later as I ask him to take a minute to receive what came, be glad that it spoke, protect it from critical voices, know how it came, and integrate it for himself before anything else is said. As he takes the time to do that I notice that his deep breathing continues.

When he returns his attention to the room I share my thoughts with him. I don't have enough scientific knowledge to explain it, and in any case I'm not sure, but perhaps in some real physiological way he has been knocking himself out, not getting enough oxygen and so going to sleep. He tells me that this fits with some other things he has been told about being a shallow breather. But my real moment of triumph comes later in the day, when he seeks me out to tell me that, even though the problem with falling asleep was one he had struggled for years trying to solve, even with professional help, since our sessions, It has not returned and, for all intents and purposes, it is gone!

FOCUSING ON THE GOOD:
SOME EXAMPLES

*originally published in The Focusing
Connection, September 1984*

IS IT POSSIBLE AND USEFUL to focus on the good
feeling, like the one that comes when the space is clear? YES!
I heard about this from Mary McDonald at a Weekend
Intensive in Chicago where we were both trainers, and had a
chance to try it out twice before the end of that weekend.

On Sunday I found myself with a participant who was
feeling good about all she done on the weekend and didn't feel
any need to focus. In fact, she was opposed to doing it because
she felt Focusing meant more getting in touch with problems.
I suggested a couple of ways that Focusing can be used to get
positive information, including this new exercise, and the idea
appealed to her. So I began to guide her through it.

I first asked her to pay attention to the good feeling and
to get the word or image for the quality (handle) of that good
feeling. When she had it I asked her to resonate it a few times,
to see if it was really right or complete. When it really fit, I
then suggested a few positive questions to choose from, such
as, "What is the best of all that /handle/?" or "What would I

like to know about all of that /handle/?" or "What would it like to tell me?" (I always suggest a few questions and let the Focuser choose the one that seems to be right for her/him.) Something came, and I asked her to take a minute to receive it. Finally I asked if she'd like to check inside to see if she was wanting to stop or if "in there" said there was the need to go on. She sensed the rightness of stopping. When we talked about what had happened I discovered that she had ended up with an answer to something that had been troubling her after all, though she had not been Focusing on it. It was how to carry away all she had gotten on the weekend and share it with all the people she knew. The image that came in answer to her question told her she could choose who she took along with her on this new path and feel OK about being selective. She was now feeling even better than before.

Later that day I worked with another participant who was feeling good about all he had done with his problems, and wondering how best to use the time. I suggested that one of the possibilities was Focusing on the good feeling and asked him to check inside as to what felt right to him at the moment. He was delighted with the idea of Focusing on the good place. Since he was right there with it, without preliminary I suggested he go inside and pay attention to the quality of it. Then when he was ready I suggested he get the handle for that quality, and he told me the word that came. As he resonated it back and forth to the felt sense another word was added and then he resonated again and a third word came. I suggested he check one more time and see if all three words were really right now, and as he did so something opened. Later he told me he was in a deeper place than he had ever been. I asked him to do the receiving step, reminding him of all the parts of it (be glad that it spoke, protect it from critical voices, know how it came, and integrate it for himself before needing to say anything). He was surprised at how quickly it had all happened and checked his watch: elapsed time, seven minutes! Upon checking inside he found he wanted to go on, so he got back in touch with the place he had come to, and I suggested some positive questions for him to choose from. He asked one inside, waited a minute, and something came. Again I guided him through receiving it and later he share with me only that it was another very important piece of what he had worked on earlier and was like a background or signpost for the very important work that was facing him and was related to the problems he had been working on all weekend. He felt wonderful. I was reminded of what Mary McDonald had said—that though you focus on the bright side of the coin, the dark side is right underneath, and often you get information about both.

MORE ON THE CRITIC AND
OTHER PARENTAL VOICES

Originally published in The Focusing Connection, March 1985

IN HER ARTICLE on "Identifying the Critic," [TFC, January, 1985], Elfie Hinterkopf writes about how important it is to be watchful for the critical voice when it comes in the Focusing process, and not to mistake it for what comes from Focusing. I would like to broaden what she says, because I find there are other voices from the head, parental in nature, often trying to be helpful, that equally get in the way of the Focusing process, and so require the same vigilance.

These parental voices, critic and others, seem to get scared at times that they will no longer be needed, or tolerated, and become frantic with suggestions and answers, none of them new.

So the speed at which something comes, and also how new and fresh versus old and familiar it is, are also clues to distinguish Focusing from the critic and "helpful" head voices:

Focusing
slow
new/unexpected

Critic/Head
immediate response
old/familiar

These two can also be distinguished by type of language. As a guide I am most watchful of these differences in language and also teach people to be cognizant of the differences in their own Focusing.

Focusing	Critic/Head
simple	complex
childlike	sophisticated
colloquial	formal
quality words	labels
sounds, movements, body postures	intellectual descriptions of sounds...

In dealing with head voices as a guide, I notice when I suggest the focuser ask a question and they give a quick, ready answer, rather than going inside to ask and wait. I bring this to the focuser's attention and say, "That is your head helping you out, so go inside and ask there instead."

When guiding I often say, following the asking suggestion, "Your head can't help you because it doesn't know the answer, which is something newer." Or I may say, "If what comes is something you already know, that is your head trying to help, so set it aside and go inside and ask again."

If when seeking a handle the person uses a word that would fit in column #2 above, I point out, "That may be your head helping you, and encourage them to look for a quality word or phrase that is simple, childlike, colloquial, such as fuzzy, jumpy, cloudy, or like someone standing on my chest; or [in Focusing on the positive] calm, peaceful, free, or like going up with a kite.

My goal is to have the focuser be able to say to themselves in response to head voices, "Oh, there it goes again," and gently but firmly set it aside and go back to what they were doing when it interrupted.

GIVING THE ENDING A CHANCE

Originally published in The Focusing Connection, January 1987

I HAVE FOUND a great bonus often awaits if an extra minute or two is taken at the end of the Focusing session. I noticed that the focuser would say it was okay to stop when I suspected their concern was that time is almost up or they felt they had taken a lot of time. They may in fact have gotten to a somewhat better place, and they sounded quieter, and yet there was no evidence of positive energy. The focuser was willing to settle for that, though I still heard some heaviness in their voice.

At such times I now suggest that they go back inside for one last full minute to see if "It" has anymore to say before they stop, or if "It" wishes to ask anything of them before they finish. Often the fresh air or positive energy is close by and just a bit of asking brings it forward. If anything does come, then of course we take another minute or two for receiving.

I have been stressing this point lately when I teach guiding. Fortunately my partner at one group session listened. So she suggested the extra minute to me when I thought I had gone as far as I could go, and time was about up. I went inside and an image that had flashed in very briefly earlier in the session suddenly completed itself in a very different form. I found myself at a very surprising (for me) spiritual place with a very different energy.

WHAT IF YOU ARE STUCK...

Originally published in The Focusing Connection, November 1987

BEING "STUCK" IN FOCUSING is a very common experience. Having been there a number of times myself, I appreciate ideas and possibilities to consider. Here are a few I've tried or heard lately.

When I go inside and I can't get in touch with what I want and no suggestion helps, it has often turned out that the little place doesn't know what it wants, because it doesn't feel safe to ask for it and is sure it couldn't get it anyway. At one such point my partner's offer to just hold me, instantly, to my surprise, found me collapsed in a puddle of my own tears. I had no idea tears were even close by.

My good friend and fellow workshop trainer Lakme Stanford, taught me a couple of good ones. Sometimes there is more than one thing, equally strong, demanding attention at the very same time and as they push against each other in the middle I feel stuck. So now I go and see what all may be there. I separate them, and can have them both, without having to choose between them, because I can make a space for each one. It's like separating two kids who were fighting, putting them in different rooms, and spending time with each one without having to pick a favorite and cause pain to the other one..

She also learned from inside, it may be that she is trying to go directly to work on the problem and it's not ready for such a direct attack. We realized it's like being taught when you were little that if the bowl of porridge is hot you get burned trying to eat it in the center. But if you eat around the edges it's cooler and more manageable. Of course if you keep eating around the edges you end up in the center which by that time has cooled down. So when an inside place feels too hot to handle, go and see what maybe close by around the edges that feel OK to be with instead.

If you have some more suggestions, my Focusing friends out there, please share them with us.

JUST SAYING HELLO

Originally published in The Focusing Connection, September 1990

THERE IS A LITTLE PLACE we talk about inside of us. We also talk to it, talk for it, talk at it, talk down to it. We may even think we are doing the right thing, because at least we are aware it is there, and we are saying so in all these ways.

The question to be considered here is how does it feel about all of these ways? In fact have we ever thought of talking it into the decision about how we talk to it or about it? Sometimes what is needed is just to say hello to it, to acknowledge its presence in this way. Often it is unaccustomed to just being acknowledged and will respond most positively to "Hello".

I hasten to add that this is not in any way intended to imply that you have to like it or accept it. Just say hello to it and see what comes next.

An illustration may be helpful. Recently I was working with someone (the first and only time), and this person said "Over here," pointing inside, "is a place that wants to give it everything it wants, and over here" (pointing to the other side of the body), "is a place that tells it it can't have everything it wants."

So I said, "What if you didn't have to tell it it can't have everything it wants, and also what if you didn't have to give it everything it wants? Would it be okay to just say hello to it? Let it know you know it is there."

The tears came, which then proceeded step by step, with my simply reflecting, to the point of finding the inner warrior, the place of power which was going to protect that person's space!

After receiving and protecting what came, the person said with surprise and new awareness, "I thought I knew what it wanted!"

LISTENING TO YOUR INNER PLACE OF WISDOM

Feature article in The Focusing Connection,
Vol. XVII, No. 3, May 2000

THE BEST GUIDE of the Focusing process is the part or place inside that knows. What does it know? It knows what is right for you in the moment.

It will never give you more than you can handle, as long as you don't allow anyone to push it, and that includes you. It is the safest authority that you will learn to trust.

So if your partner, or any other guide or teacher, makes a suggestion to you, check and see if it feels right to do it, before you try it. Then let your guide know if it doesn't feel right. That is safer and also more productive than just trying to do something that doesn't feel OK, and not letting the guide know you are sensing a place that says No. If you sense a place that says No, that place needs you to back up and be with it, before doing any moving forward.

For example, let's look at "saying hello." When you become aware of any felt sense (body sense), saying hello to it is just acknowledging to it that you are noticing that it is there. It does not mean you are happy to see it, or that you like it, or that it is a good time for it to show up, or that you accept it.

And yet, knowing all that, it still may not feel right for you to say Hello. When that happens, it is time to be curious about what is in the way. This is useful whenever anything doesn't feel right for you to do, even something you may want to do and know you would like having done.

Let me emphasize again: this principle is above whoever may be guiding you, a more experienced Focuser, a teacher you respect and want to learn from, even Gene Gendlin himself. No matter who is suggesting it, if it doesn't feel right to your inner place, don't do the suggestion--but be curious about what is in the way.

A man who has been attending workshops and Changes groups for almost two years, spoke up recently to say he doesn't like saying Hello. Having just read Reva Bernstein's worthy article on her five A's (TFC, January 2000) gave him the idea he might be able to do something different here. And of course that is always a possibility.

But first I suggested that we go and see about he place that says No to saying Hello. Being with it with wonder and curiosity, he discovered that that part of him felt that if someone says Hello to you, something is also expected of it in return. So it said, "Leave me alone." Here was new information about how it felt about expectations.

At other times we have discovered that someone may not be able to say Hello because they can't find the place to say Hello to. So then we can know that it may be hiding and that is what is important to be with at that moment.

So whenever anything, even something you need to do but isn't getting done, is stuck or blocked from action, then go and find with wonder and curiosity what is in the way.

Verifying the Process

The moment comes when we are Focusing and we feel ready for asking a question of the part that has a particular feeling or sense to it. Asking, perhaps, what is needed.

There are three ways to prepare for this moment, to make it more likely that the answer comes from the part.

First, knowing it has a reason that it feels that way and that it has a story to tell.

Second, knowing that the story is more than what we already know. Also, that it may not be ready to speak to us just then, or that the story may come in small pieces or steps.

Third, we need to bring the Focusing attitude of asking and waiting with wonder and curiosity rather than asking and answering by telling it what we do know. This can be one of the most difficult parts of learning Focusing. All that we do know about ourselves probably has a lot of truth to it, and our mind is very quick to tell us what that is. But it hasn't helped to resolve the problem. So when the mind answers, we can appreciate and acknowledge that our mind wants to be helpful. Then we can ask again and wait for something more or different or newer than is like a breath of fresh air.

So how can we tell, when an answer does come to our question, where it is coming from? Since what we already know comes quickly, sounding like The Truth, we can then ask, "How did it feel when it came to us?" Now we are back in touch with our inner place that knows. If it feels just the same as when we asked, or if it feels heavy or discouraging as when we are getting put down or dumped on, then we can be sure it is not an answer from the inside place.

When it feels a little lighter, or is a bit of a surprise,

because you wouldn't have thought of it just then, or is a newer way of seeing something and has some good energy with it, then we can tell it is an answer we were awaiting. That is the time to stop and receive it.

Receiving has three parts: appreciating what it just gave us; protecting it from our mind's tendency to jump in and question what does it mean, or what are we going to do about it, or wanting to analyze it; and marking the new piece so we can find it again by noticing how we got to it or retracing our steps briefly.

"Am I really Focusing?" is a common question when someone is first learning the process. Noticing how it feels when something comes is the way to know--a way you can depend on always.

Ending the Focusing Process

When the Focusing time is almost up, there is a rich potential possible. Rather than just stopping and leaving the inside place abruptly, there are other choices we can make.

Letting the inside place know by actually telling it that it is almost time to stop, and asking it to find a right stopping place, is one choice. That respects the place we are keeping company with and hoping to learn from. That also acknowledges that it is very capable and can determine what would be a right way to stop.

Another possibility, which often adds to the session: As you are giving it notice about time running out, ask it if there is anything else it would like you to know before you leave it. Then just waiting and wondering. It doesn't have to say anything and may not do so. If something does come freshly there, it is important to take another few minutes to receive it.

AFTER HELLO: THE BRIDGE TO RIGHT RELATIONSHIP

Originally published in The Focusing Connection, May 2002

MANY YEARS AGO, while guiding Focusers, I began suggesting they say "hello" to inner parts of themselves, to say "hello" just as they would if it were another person. Recently I've become aware that what needs to follow "hello" is common courtesy: this provides the bridge to the right relationship.

So how did it all start? A Focuser said to me, "Part of me wants to tell it that it can't have everything it wants. At the same time, another part of me wants to give it everything it wants." I asked, "What if you didn't have to tell it that it couldn't have everything it wants, and also didn't have to give it everything it wants? How would it feel to just simply say 'hello' to it?" As the Focuser took my suggestion inside, it felt right. So as I continued to just listen and reflect, it led the Focuser to discover the long-lost warrior within. It was a major step with wonderful energy now available.

I had noticed that we talk to, talk at, talk about the inside places without ever listening to them. After some time I began to suggest the Focuser check to notice if the inner place heard the "hello," and how it felt about it. If it heard, how did it respond? Was it pleased, or perhaps it was afraid if it heard the "hello," something more might be expected of it? Maybe we couldn't even find it to say "hello" to it because it was hiding.

And then I came to look at how we say "hello," and I concluded it was just as if some person entered the room. Saying "hello" doesn't imply you are happy to see the person, though you might be, nor does it imply that you like the person, though you might. It doesn't even mean you wouldn't prefer to be left alone in peace and quiet at that time. It is just courteous to acknowledge directly to the person that you noticed them come in. It would be rude and unkind to remark to a third person instead, "Oh, by the way, so and so just came in."

And now to take it a step further, perhaps you notice the person's expression revealing something of what they are feeling, such as upset, angry, sad, excited, happy, or down. Or perhaps they might tell you why they came; something happened at work or with a friend. Common courtesy requires that you acknowledge to them directly what you noticed or what they told you. In a Focusing way that happens by reflecting back to them to see if you have it correctly. Starting the reflection by saying "you" is most direct. For example, reflecting "You are really upset by what just happened at work," or "You are sad that your friend hasn't the time to get together anymore."

This idea applies equally to all inner parts, including the one some refer to as the critic, even though that one may specialize in pointing out one's weakness in its way of attempting to be helpful. So you might be reflecting to it, "So, you are disappointed and angry because I didn't speak up for myself when that happened at work."

However, as always, noticing what feels right in the moment is primary. So, if it feels right to say "hello" to and reflect to those inner places directly and with common courtesy as though they were other persons, you can build the bridge to the right relationship - to your inside place with all its parts.

FOCUSING RECOLLECTIONS: THE FIRST "HELLO" AND MORE

FEATURE ARTICLE in The Focusing Connection, Vol. XXIV, No. 2 March 2007

Recently Bebe Simon, legendary Focusing teacher from Chicago, visited me and was telling stories about the early days of Eugene Gendlin's workshops, when she was one of his first assistants who would "sit with" people and help them find Focusing. Her stories were so engaging that I asked if I could transcribe some of them for the Connection. They also illustrate important points about Focusing we'd all do well to remember. —AWC

I remember the first time I ever asked someone to say "Hello" to something. She was a woman from Canada, I remember very clearly. I was sitting with her and she said, "Part of me wants to tell it that it can't have everything it wants. And part of me wants to give it everything it wants."

I didn't know what she was referring to, because we didn't start with a story. She just said that, those two sentences, after she started Focusing.

So I said to her, "What if you didn't have to give it everything it wants. And what if you didn't have to tell it, it can't have everything it wants. What if you just said hello to it."

I don't know where it came from that I said that, it just came to me. It's like we talk down to it, we talk at it, but we don't ever listen to it.

After that I don't think I did much guiding at all. She went on to find her inner Warrior. She was not going to let anybody in again unless she wanted them in. She got so strong, she found such a wonderful resolution.

I really did not do much after that. Just listened. I didn't have to do anything. She took it and ran with it. As for saying "Hello," I wouldn't forget to use it again, when it was that great!

The second story is about my friend in California, an experienced Focuser. We used to listen to each other whenever I visited her. I remember one time, she just spit out what came, said it so quickly. I said, "Wait, better if you don't say it right away, and just have it for you first." And then next time I saw her, she said to me, "You know what it told me?" and she made a face, like a pout. "It said, I didn't want you to tell her."

There's the proof of it, what we always said, best not to say it right away, because it might not want you to say it, and you have to ask it if it's OK to say it. It wasn't anything personal, that I remember.

Then there was the time with Jay S. Later we became really good friends, but then I didn't even know him, and he asked to work with me, I don't know why. He sat down and said, "Well, I guess I have to tell the story." Like he was sick of telling it.

And I said, "No, you don't have to tell the story." And he looked at me like I'm crazy. I said, "No, you don't need to. You know the story. Could you just go inside and be with the place that it's about?"

And that was when, after just a little bit, he caught his breath and said "Oh! It's on my side!" And then he gasped again, and said, "Oh! I thought it was the enemy!" That was the big thing. Of course I reflected that.

At the end, when he said goodbye to me, he said, "You don't know this, but I'm saying goodbye to you in a new voice." Later I found out he'd been a stutterer. We didn't talk about that, I'm just guessing that might be what his session was about. People don't realize, they don't need to tell the story.

I always tell people, "The inside place likes little words." This next one is an example of that. There was a psychologist in New York who was brilliant at observation. He could take apart what he saw like no one I've ever seen. Really amazing. But he talked a lot. He was always explaining what he saw. People didn't even want to be with him in the groups because he talked so much.

I worked with him, we did Focusing, and little by little, as I cut down on what he could say and what I had to say, he got the idea he just loved the little words. He loved the simple language. That changed him. People said to me, "What did you do to him?"

One day after a long period of time of not hearing from him, I got a phone call. What a gift.

He said he had a patient who had panic attacks. That's the only reason she was there. After they'd been working together a while, she had a panic attack in the office. He said to her, "Boy, that's scary." And she pulled herself up to her full dignity and said, "That's a little girl word."

He said very softly and warmly, "Yes it is."

And the dam broke. She cried. She said she knew to do it with her 9-year-old at home but it never dawned on her to do it with herself—to understand that there's a little person inside.

He said, "Bebe, it happens all the time now. Thank you for the little words."

I always knew the word "accept" was a problem, I never knew why. I said so to Peter Campbell once, and he said, "I know why. Too many shoulds."

There was somebody who came to one of the workshops, he had come from a month at a very intensive deep meditation retreat, about a month before. He said he had been trying to accept something ever since then, and he was having trouble with it. I said "What if you didn't have to accept it. Could you just say hello to it?"

Well! Before we were finished he was holding it gently, lovingly, protecting it, all the acceptance from his heart. No shoulds.

It was so beautiful to watch how loving he was with it.

So I prefer to acknowledge, that's all. I say, "Let it know you know it's there."

THE POWER OF HELLO
BY ANN WEISER CORNELL

Originally published in The Focusing Connection,
Vol. XXIV, No. 2 March 2007

IT WAS FROM BEBE SIMON that I first learned to invite Focusers to say "Hello" to what they were feeling. I remember how the beautiful simplicity of this move excited my imagination. I wondered, what makes this such a perfect invitation? And the answer was one of the streams that flowed into the development of Inner Relationship Focusing.

Bebe's story (see page one) of the first time she ever used this invitation is a perfect example of how powerful it is. The Focuser said, "Part of me wants to tell it that it can't have everything it wants. And part of me wants to give it everything it wants." The Focuser is caught in an inner conflict and can only see two choices, but neither of those choices are *just being with* the "it" inside.

The companion *could* say "Maybe you could just be with it," but very likely that's a hard place to find from where the Focuser is right now. Instead Bebe said, about the two options, "What if you didn't have to do [A]. And what if you didn't have to do [B]. What if you just said hello to it." We can feel the graceful simplicity of this. Saying "Hello" is a non-doing. It takes the place of doing. At the same time, it is relational. By saying "Hello" I come into relationship, into contact with what I'm saying "Hello" to.

This is the amazing power of Hello: by saying "Hello" to something, we come into contact with it – and *no more*. It's a contact with no agenda, no preference, no impatience or pulling back.

Why is that no-agenda kind of contact so important? Because the felt sense needs that. It needs that special combination of company and space. If we pull or push on it, it will fight or hide... and neither fighting nor hiding lets it be what it needs to be: itself.

With this simple and elegant move of saying "Hello" a whole world opens. It's the world of trust in what is, trust that what is here has its own unfolding, its own next steps, its own life-forward process.

And there is more: saying "Hello" to what we feel is an alignment along an axis of curiosity, respect, interest, compassion, and, ultimately, love. On this axis, "hello" is a first move that implies and begins a movement toward all the rest. "Hello" is exactly not interfering, judging, resisting, arguing, escaping, evaluating, analyzing...

"Hello" is the first move toward respect, compassion, love, etc. and yet it is not those either... not yet. So it is safe; it can be dared. As Bebe always says, "'Hello' is not 'I love you'."

How "Hello" Leads to the Concept of Presence

As I pondered this amazingly simple move, and tried it myself, I came to see that by saying "Hello" to something that I felt, I was *being* the one who could say "Hello" to it. Saying "Hello" was relational. In a subtle but powerful way it lit up both sides of the relationship – both the one receiving the "hello" and the one giving it. I was saying "Hello," so I was not interfering, judging, resisting, and analyzing. And if interfering, judging, resisting, etc. arose, I could say "Hello" to *that*! No matter what, I could remain the one who said "Hello." This was powerful. This was revolutionary.

I taught this in my Focusing classes... and my students began to ask me, *"Who* is it who is saying 'Hello'? What part of me is that?" I didn't know the answer... but I could feel that calling it a "part" was wrong somehow. I say "Hello"; not part of me, but me.

So at the very start of the Focusing session my whole self is moving into relationship with my felt experiences, to become their listener, to be there with no agenda except to keep company. And I don't have to do this by "finding" the one in me who can do that; I can just say "Hello."

When Saying "Hello" is Hard

Sometimes I work with someone who has a hard time saying "Hello." They will say something like this: "I don't know how to do that. The anxiety feels like all of me. I don't feel anything separate from that."

Then I will invite body sensing. The body helps us *localize* felt experience. What at first feels "all over" begins to feel centered in a location.

I say, "OK. Yes, it feels like all of you. So maybe you could notice where in your body you feel it the *most* right now."

The Focuser will take a moment to sense, and then say, "In

my stomach" or "In my chest," for example.

Now I will use the help of their hands. "Maybe you could let a gentle hand go there. Just rest it on that place. Like with your hand, you're saying, 'Hello I'm with you' to that place."

I've never known this to fail to evoke a sense of gentle company... and it often brings great relief.

When Saying "Hello" isn't Helpful

There are some times when saying "Hello" is not helpful. Those are the times when what is felt is still too vague. In the Focuser's experience, what is felt is like a puff of smoke which could be blown away by a strong breath. In such cases, "Hello" may be too strong. After being invited to say "Hello," the Focuser will say, "It's gone," or "I don't feel it any more." When the felt sense is vague and not very strong, I would suggest just staying with it, trusting that with time it will become strong enough for more connection.

Although I use it in many sessions, I find that saying "Hello" remains most helpful in those times of inner conflict, as in Bebe's story. When the Focuser is identified with something, either a feeling or (more often) a feeling *about* the feeling, "Hello" is so effective for bringing Presence, it's like a little miracle. I'm grateful every day for this miracle.

ARTICLES PUBLISHED
IN OTHER VENUES

FOCUSING FOR LIFE

Originally published in The Monthly Aspectarian, January 2001

FOCUSING - A POTENT MEANS of being at ease in the present

"Something about Focusing caught my attention," my friend James said. "I was into major transition-- breakup of a marriage, what to do for my future life. I was either stuck in the past thinking of what had been, or toying with the future of what might be. Then Focusing taught me how to stay in the present moment instead. Whew! What a relief! ... not just in my head or my heart, but relief in my body ... a clear knowing that something had shifted."

Every child comes into the world with a sense (you could call it a blueprint) of how life would be for them if all went just right. It rarely happens that way. The survival instinct enables the child to adapt to life as they find it. Some learn to please, be nice or quiet, or to help take care of others. Some rebel, either openly or passively. So the pattern of life is chosen. In my case, after many years of therapy, I discovered I had "sold my soul down the river" to please and be nice. And that was with a two-parent, loving, well-intentioned family. However, the blueprint of knowing what "just right" would feel like remains to let us know when something isn't right. Focusing teaches us how to be present to this inner guide we call a felt sense. We learn to notice and acknowledge a body sense about anything and everything in our life, where here to fore we had been used to ignoring it, or dismissing it, or not feeling it at all.

Focusing resulted from research conducted by Professor Eugene Gendlin (pronounce with a soft G) at the University of Chicago. He and his colleagues wanted to find out why therapy so often failed to make a real difference in people's lives. They found it was not due to a difference in method or technique but that what successful therapy clients did was something inside themselves. As Gendlin says, "This internal act'is a way of approaching any problem or situation. It becomes an internal source that is consulted many times a day. I am using it right now, in the process of writing this book" (p. 4, Focusing by Eugene T. Gendlin, Ph.D, Bantam Books).

Finding deeper meaning is also enabled by focusing on the positive things of life. Let's try it right now with the Love Exercise. Are you sitting comfortably in your chair? Take a moment to do that. Now pick something you love, a picture, a gift, an activity, anything except person or a pet. Now think of why you love it. Now imagine seeing it, or doing it or using it. As you do so, let your attention be in your body. Can you notice the feltsense of being with the thing you love? Take your time. Is there a word or phrase that would describe the body sense of being with it? When you have one, check and see if it really matches with the body sense. Now just ask, and wait, and wonder: what about the thing you love makes that feltsense? Wait for some new idea to come. When it does, notice how it felt. Then just spend some time with it so you get to keep it.

I am reminded of someone who chose to focus on her needlepoint work. She knew she loved the beauty of what she was creating. When she focused on it in this way, she discovered it was the peacefulness it brought as she worked, and yet she had not been aware of it before. In a second opportunity to do the Love Exercise at a later time, she again picked this work. This time it came to her that she was sewing herself together. A true revelation!

As Gendlin says, "General descriptions do not convey focusing. It differs from the general attention we pay to feelings because it begins with the body and occurs in the zone between the conscious and the unconscious. Most people don't know that a bodily sense of any topic can be invited to come into that zone, and that one can enter into such a sense. At first it is only a vague discomfort, but soon it becomes a distinct sense with which one can work, and in which one can sort out many strands" (p. 1, Focusing-oriented Psychotherapy: a Manual of the Experiential Method by Eugene Gendlin, Guilford Press).

Gendlin invented a method for teaching people to focus. For the natural focuser, how to use it more; for others, how to rediscover this natural ability to listen to this inward bodily awareness.

Learning the skill of listening empathically to others is the way to learn to listen to oneself that way. As we take the part of the listener, our goal is for the person who is focusing to feel heard. This is often a real challenge at first, and is most satisfying to both people when it's done well. This special kind of listening is done with reflecting [saying back in different words] what we hear to see if we have the way it was meant. It is done without analyzing, advice, argument, editing or adding one's own experience. This does not come easily for many people. Listening may have seldom been offered by parents, teachers, loving friends and family. So it is a new skill to be developed.

One of the special qualities of focusing is its unlimited usefulness. If you find listening difficult, empathy unavailable, and many other things you would like to do but feel stuck in attaining, you can always focus on what is in the way.

Focusing is helpful for improving the quality of life and our interaction with others. As Marilyn Ferguson said in her introduction to the book Focusing, it can help to "discover the richness in others by learning to listen. It looks at the potential for a new kind of relationship and a new kind of society."

Therapists and clients have used focusing to enhance the therapy process. Others as well, seeking renewal and growth in their lives, have used it personally and professionally in teaching, in business, in the arts ... the full range of human endeavor. Focusing will "enable you to find and change where your life is stuck, cramped, hemmed in, slowed down, and it will enable you to change -- to live from a deeper place than just your thoughts and feelings" (pg. 4, Focusing).

When Focusing happens, it feels good, "like fresh air." We know that everything you feel has a reason it feels that way --- and furthermore, that it has a story to tell. Your inner place will not give you any more than you can handle at any time. This is a built-in safety factor.

Another unusual aspect of the focusing process is that it offers total privacy. A friend, Robert, tells of asking some helping professionals why, in order to get help, it is sometimes necessary to say what one doesn't feel ready to share. The response was, "Because that is the way it is." Then he found focusing, and knew it was possible to keep contents private and still get help. That way you don't have to wait to get to know or trust the listener. If you aren't going to say any more than you wish to, and that that is just fine, it shortens the time in which one can deal with deeper issues.

So James said, "I tried combining it with all these other things I know, various therapeutic avenues, meditation, dream work, visualization ...wow! I found I could enhance these other methods for personal development. By now I'm hooked ... I want to know more ... I found the more I exercised my ability to check inside, the more able I was to know what I really wanted. I felt my inside place come alive, I noticed changes in the way I behaved. The more I spent time this way, the more my body, my mind, and my spirit knew I was more fully who I am because of my practice of focusing."

IT NEEDS TO MAKE SENSE...

by Bebe Simon, interviewed and transcribed by Rob Foxcroft
Edited by Bebe Simon, Bala Jaison, and Paula Nowick

*A later version of this article was originally
published in the Focusing Folio, 200x.*

IT NEEDS TO MAKE SENSE...

*ROB: The first Focusing person I ever spoke to was Mary
McGuire. This was in January 1988. When Mary encouraged
me to come to Chicago for some Focusing courses, she asked Bebe
Simon if I might stay with her. In this way, I came to have a home
in Chicago, where I have always been made welcome; and there I
learned Focusing at all times of the day and night.*

*So when Bala Jaison asked me to interview Bebe for the Folio
about aging, I was delighted to invite her to share her stories,
her experience and her wisdom. I listened to Bebe's thoughts and
memories for an hour or two during the recent Focusing Conference
in Pforzheim. But we never spoke about aging. Does this mean that
Bebe's reflections are irrelevant to this Folio?*

*Of course not. As Bebe looks back over thirty years of Focusing
and eighty-five years of living, I invite you to think of her words as
a vast Receiving step – the sixth step in Gene Gendlin's Focusing
model. Receiving has a peculiar poignancy in late life. But Bebe is*

*not only receiving. There is also forward movement here – carrying
forward – something youthful, very much alive and growing,
something decidedly forward looking.*

*What was going forward as we talked was tender and self-
directing. I was not about to shape it. Bebe had her own path.
Mostly I listened very simply, in the way I like to listen, though
with the special tenderness of long friendship. As you read, you
will maybe get a sense of deepening process, of emotional levels
emerging and shifting as our talk goes on. You will witness a
person aging with Focusing, a life more and more fully human,
and rich in memory.*

*In these stories, I hope you will feel the depth of years and
experience in a dear friend and colleague; who never, she tells me,
thinks about aging, never about getting old, never dwells upon
her years of life. And I think Bebe will always be young. When
I was watching her dancing with Christian, at the conference
in Pforzheim, I was not thinking about aging. He was the most
gallant, most graceful man on the floor; and she the most youthful,
most radiant woman. So I was thinking of the sixteen year old
Natasha at her first ball, in Tolstoy's famous novel. Is this what
Bebe is telling us about aging, after thirty Focusing years: that with
Focusing, you will always be young?*

*Note: Since my words are in italics, I have used underlining
for emphasis.*

*Rob: I thought you might like to begin by telling me the bit of
the story I don't know at all. How did you first come to be sitting
down with somebody learning to do Focusing? And who was it?
And all those things.*

Bebe: After many years of therapy, of more than one kind,
I was informed by a member of my family that there was a

new kind of therapy in the paper that day. When I went home I saw in the *Chicago Tribune* an interview with Gene Gendlin. The article said that there would be two upcoming Saturday afternoon introductory sessions at the university – and Gene would be there. I was about to go away for a vacation, and I thought, "Oh! This is Tuesday, for this Saturday. It's probably all filled up, but I will call, anyway."

So I call up and they say, "Oh no, that's fine. Come." And it was only fifteen dollars for the afternoon, so you know how long ago that was! It was something like '79, because the paperback edition of the book, *Focusing*, had just come out. The workshop organizers wanted to get us all to go to bookstores, to get them to stock the paperback.

I had a strong feeling of wanting to go and learn what this was. So I went there on that Saturday, and it was, I think, Ann Weiser Cornell who was doing an introduction for Gene – and then he spoke.

I very often ask questions, and I like to sit up front. And when I asked a question he said to me, "Did I answer your question?" My face hadn't changed. That's how he knew he hadn't answered my question; but I didn't know that. "Wow. He's up there, and he was able to ask that – very interesting!" And so I said, "Well, sort of…" and he said, "Ask it again"… (Bebe laughs.)

Rob: So Gene Gendlin said, "Ask it again."

Bebe: Yes. So I asked it again, and then he answered. And I was very impressed with that, particularly, that he would have such an open attitude.

They were then talking about a program that they were going to be offering shortly, but since I would be away, I would not be able to be there for that. So I let them know that I would be interested in the future, and by the time I came back in the Spring, they were planning three Saturdays, each one by a different person, and in a different place. One was at Reva Bernstein's house, and that was the only one that Gene Gendlin would attend, and I wanted to be where he was, so I signed up for that one.

There was a woman at that time who knew she was moving out of the state to the west coast. She had taken the program while I was away. Now she wanted to take in as much as she could to get as much as she could; and I wanted to practice. We both worked down town. We were able to arrange to be at a university, maybe Roosevelt, in the cafeteria, where we could have a meeting at five o'clock, and do some of this work. She thought she would be guiding me. She did not expect me to be able to guide her, but I was already able to do that. So we had several exchanges, once or twice a week – and that, so to speak, was my introduction to Focusing.

Then I heard there was a Changes Group, involving Gene. I was interested enough to go, though it wasn't the most convenient location for me. The lady who was hosting was a nurse, and every week we went to her house. But the way Focusing was done in that Changes group was so different from what I was familiar with. First, what they did was guide the whole group, to get them ready for Focusing. And if you got a sense of what you wanted to Focus on, you then picked someone who was just sitting there, to listen to you out of the group.

"Would you listen to me?" – "Yes" – "OK, then I will work with you."

This was my first experience with Changes. It seems to me that we always stayed in the big group. And as I continued to go there, I may have known then, I'm not sure, that someday I wanted something like that in my area – that I would want to have such a group – but not necessarily the way they did it.

Meanwhile, the weekend workshops had started. And it was quite expensive. It was $250. And since Focusing was not part of my work life, there was no one else to pay for it. So it was a big decision as to whether or not to spend that much money. But the lady who was hosting the Changes group also wanted to go, and eventually we both went to that weekend.

The weekend was very different from those previous three days we had already done. And they were supposed to give you each one or two new Focusing students to work with, for a research project. You would guide somebody in Focusing, and the researchers would then have some record of this work. And I remember, when Gene was there, I said to him, "How do I know if I'm doing well enough to get a student? You know, am I succeeding in this course?" And being Gene, he was very casual about it. Oh, he's sure it would be fine, yes. (We both laugh.) There was no sense that he was really judging it. He didn't seem to have any questions about it. Why, I don't know. So I did get one person, and showed that person Focusing, to some extent. I don't really remember how well it went, but I did enjoy it.

And then I heard that Gene was going to present to the Illinois Psychological Association. There would be maybe two or three hundred people in a large room, and he asked all the people that were then interested in his work to come and help him. Reva and Ann may have been there. I don't remember everybody, but it was just an informal invitation, you know, "Will you come and help Gene?" – "Sure" – and of course Gene takes a room full of people, lots of chairs, and tells them to move into little groups, breaking up the whole room. He had us going around from group to group. They were supposed to be listening to each other, and we were supposed to be there to help them, if they needed it. So I went around, and if someone needed help, I stopped and saw what the problem was, and how I might help.

Not too long after that I was asked if I would come and help at the regular weekend workshops. Yes, I would – I was delighted that they asked me. Most of the young people there at the time were either psychology students, or had already studied with Gene at the University of Chicago. I felt that Reva and I were probably the only ones who weren't in that advanced category – it seemed to me advanced, you know.

But they did ask me to come. I remember going, and there were some young women from out of town. So since I was available, I asked them: Where they would they like to go for lunch and dinner, during the workshop? So we'd go out, just spending some time together, because I knew the places, and whatever they liked or wanted – I knew where to suggest. So we had a very nice, cosy relationship over the weekend. And at one point this young woman said to me, "Bebe, how long have you been doing this?" and I said, "It's my first time." She looked at me (Bebe is laughing) as if I were crazy. She was quite startled. I think she thought I was more experienced than I was. I said that I loved Focusing. I had such a good time. As it ended, Gene passed by, and I said, "Gene, I want you to know, I gave a lot, but I got much more than I gave." And he said, "That's as it should be."

For me it was an opening that was beyond anything I had ever experienced. It was very exciting that I could work so easily with people like that.

Well, after that I knew that what we were doing at that Changes group was not satisfactory. Unfortunately, you didn't have to have much experience with Focusing to come to the Changes group, and some people were not even interested in what I had just learned at my weekend workshops, such as guiding techniques. I went, and a friend of mine was going with me, and without knowing how to ask, exactly, I just started to guide her – and it worked. But the people there were not interested in what I had just learned. They didn't want to know. They were not impressed with the new developments in Focusing. Well, then I knew that I would not be able to stay in this Changes group very long. It was not what I wanted. I found what I wanted to do – it was exciting – and I wanted more of it.

So, sometime after that, Ruth Arkiss, who was at that time heading up the Focusing office, informed me that there was going to be a workshop in Boston about building community, and that I might be interested because I wanted to have the Changes Group at my home. The workshop was run by Kathy McGuire and her (then) husband, Zack Boukydis. They had rented this whole house for the workshop. We had the kitchen, we made the food; everything took place in this one house – we had the use of it for five or six days.

I had a cousin who lived in Boston, and she met me at the airport. I had gotten all dressed up for the airplane flight. My idea was: "I have to look proper when I'm coming into this group." So I showed up in my dress-up clothes and earrings, but everyone else was in jeans! Of course, they had come in cars because they lived close-by in that area, and I was the only one who looked so formal.

The house had dormitories, small rooms, for maybe three or four. You were supposed to pick a place for yourself, put your things down, and make yourself comfortable. Well, there was a room, and nobody seemed to be there, so I choose that place and I put my things down, and I guess it was at night when someone else – turned out it was Gladys – had also come into that room.

So when she saw me she said, "Praise the Lord!" (We both laugh.) And I thought, "What do you say to a person like that? How am I going to even talk to her? How are we going to be in the same room? We don't talk the same language at all. That's going to be a problem." But I did my exercise in the morning, and she did her meditation, her prayer, whatever… and it turned out we got along great! Really great!

Now Kathy had written a manual about Building Supportive Community – which also talked about Changes groups. And I kept telling the group – and they were getting somewhat irritated – "That's really not Focusing like that." I know my impression (to them) was that I knew better than they did about Focusing. And eventually they asked me to present something or talk about it – to tell them what it was that I knew. Gladys too said, "You're always saying, 'Well, that's not what I know'." So I did show them, and they liked it. And I was so pleased that it went over well.

By the end of the week, they had us go around, as a parting activity, and say something about each person in the group, that you had noticed or appreciated about them. So when it was Gladys' turn she went around the circle, and she had really observed everyone, and had lovely things to say about each person – she was really amazing. And then I thought to myself, "She's not got anything left to say to me. She's said everything there is you could say to the other people in the circle. What will she say to me?" And when she came to me, she said, "Bebe, I love you." I was so touched. We were already so deeply connected.

When it was over and I went home, there was someone that I knew, Sandy, who wanted to know more about Focusing, and I liked her, and I said if she would agree to come every Tuesday, we would then be a group. In case anybody wanted to come, we would put out the word that we had a group. Otherwise I would just be Focusing with her. I would show her what I could about Focusing, and she agreed to that. So for quite some time she came every week, and we started what we called 'a group', and we made it known that people were welcome to come – but in time she moved away.

Then, after Sandy, there was someone else. She was the best person in the whole world; I loved her so much. You know who it was? It was Lakme. *Then Lakme Stanford, later Lakme something else.* Yes, yes. Now she's Lakme Elior.

She was working downtown, and she was going west to her family every Tuesday. So it was not inconvenient for her to come, since I was in that direction. I arranged with her that if she would come every week and make that commitment, we would Focus together; and then we could say we have 'a group'. And she did that for a very long time. Some people did come, and sometimes they'd come one time and didn't come again; and sometimes they came more. That was the start of the Changes group. That's how it all began.

And that was very good for me – much better to have it at home. I didn't have to go to a church, which is where the Hyde Park group met, and where you had to have keys and so on. It was easy, the whole thing was very easy, to have it in my own home. That's how it began.

I continued to go to the weekend workshops. Ten months of the year. Unless I was out of town, I was there every single time. We did not get paid. I say it was like having free supervision. And although I learned, I found out that Gene was not doing what Peter Campbell and Ed McMahon were doing with the people that were helping them. They would talk to their trainers after the weekend, you know – to find out how was it for them?

Some of our people were working with Ed and Pete, as well as with us. One was Dave Young. And he would tell us things that he learned from them, that really interested me – and this happened often enough, that I got curious to find out more. Ed and Pete used to assign one person to you for the weekend – each little group would be one person's group. And I said, "Look, I don't want to be with one of the people I know. That's no novelty. I want to be with one of the priests." So Dave said OK, he could arrange it. And when I was going to the first weekend, Gene asked me to take them the book, *Let Your Body Interpret Your Dreams*, which had just come out. I took it to them as a gift from Gene, whom they knew.

In one session with Pete, something was said about 'accepting', and I said to him, "I don't use that word. I don't know why, but…" …he said (she laughs), "I know why. The church is full of, 'You <u>should</u> accept'." And so I really felt very connected to him – and part of it was that he always talked about the "Judaeo-Christian" background, and I always felt it was like...he knew I was there, too.

He included you, with your Jewish inheritance.

Yes, that was very, very special to me. And at the end, they conducted a mass. I didn't always sit in. But one time Peter was in his robes, and I said, "Can you hug a priest with robes?" "Oh, absolutely!" He was so warm, so welcoming, and I also learned certain little stories from them that I still use, that I like very much.

Could you tell one?

Well, the one that I use the most was about the tapestry. If you picture a tapestry on the wall, and you shrink yourself down to a tiny, tiny ant-sized creature, and you just crawl up the wall and hop on, it doesn't matter where, because the threads are all interconnected, all interwoven, so it doesn't matter where you start. Just hop on and follow the thread. And I always thought that was special. So I use that.

I'm also reminded now, that Gene used to allow for time that he could spend with someone after a workshop, if it was needed, because he never wanted anyone to be left going home in a bad place. There was one woman that I worked with, and evidently she had asked him for time afterward, but at the end, when he spoke to her, she said, "Oh I don't need it. I worked with Bebe." Well, I was a little bit taken aback, you know. But Gene said he got to know, from others' feedback, how it was – working with me.

Another time there was a friend of Gene's at a workshop, who came from far away – Alaska. It was a husband and wife and Gene knew the husband. He was a *big* man, a little too heavy maybe – and he tells me, when we sit down, he wants me to know that he has a problem. He tends to fall asleep when he sits down. He said he had narcolepsy. But that didn't mean anything to me, because I didn't know anything about narcolepsy. So I worked with him for a little bit, and I said something about the <u>quality</u> of his felt sense. So he paid attention, inside, then he said, "Relaxing" – "Oh", I said, "Is that the handle?" And he said, "No".

And suddenly I knew. I said, "Oh, that's the answer before the question." And he said, "Yes. That's right!" (In other words, he had skipped the handle, resonating and asking steps, and jumped straight from the felt sense to the felt shift.)

At some point, his wife spoke up about his being a shallow breather. But I didn't know any of that. I wasn't picking up on that. I didn't see it. I don't know that I would have known if I saw it. So that was interesting – and the next time, he said he wasn't falling asleep.

And that's even more interesting.

Yeah, but I didn't talk to him after that. I don't know if it lasted. At the end of that session, Gene walked in, and the man said, "She's good!" – and he said, "Yes I know." – and I say, "How do you know? You never saw me work." I was quite annoyed that he never seemed to know what I was doing. He said, "I know. I hear." And they went off to lunch. We'd had a very good experience that stayed with me forever.

There were some other interesting people that I remember. There was a woman who told me that <u>part</u> of her wants to say it can't have everything it wants, and <u>part</u> of her wants to give it everything it wants. And I heard something there: that you're talking down to it, about it, at it, you're never listening to it. So then I said to her, "What if you didn't have to give it everything it wants, and what if you also didn't have to tell it, it can't get everything it wants. What if you just said 'Hello' to it?" – "Oh!" – So then she did.

I did some reflection after that – just saying back to her what I had taken in, what I had heard. I didn't do much guiding. It didn't seem to be needed. It just kept moving along, and by the end she had found her warrior, and was not going to allow anyone to intrude again without her permission. So it was obvious she had known intrusion at some earlier time – and now it could not happen again to her in that way. And so we learned the value of saying "Hello".

Then there's another time I recall so fondly: Ann had set up a Treasure Maps just before the Canadian conference, and I was a participant. On the second day Ann said, "Oh, by the way, 'Hello' comes from Bebe" – and this woman is incredulous: "'Hello' comes from Bebe!!!???" (Bebe is laughing again.) I just sat there grinning, you know, not saying anything, but tickled pink. That was something I will never forget – the way she said that. Total shock. But Ann has always been very gracious about acknowledging other people.

And it seems to me I'm talking too much.

Well, maybe we've finished a piece of the story. That's the story of your beginnings, to the point where you even began to be recognised as a person who can give some knowledge back.

Then there was a friend in California. I went there every year to spend time with my friends and relatives there, and I would always arrange to see her. We would have a meal and do a little Focusing together. As I remember, she was talking –

nothing very personal – but as something came to her she just said it. And I said, "I have found that sometimes that place inside doesn't like to say it right away. It's better to wait and see if *it* would say, 'It's OK to tell her'" – "Oh!" – She hadn't thought about that. Later she said to me, "Do you know what *it* said to me?" – with a pouting mouth – "I didn't <u>want</u> you to tell her." So that validated what I had suspected. It's not OK. I tell people, "Don't say it. First have it for you; and then see if it's OK to say it." It's OK not to say it. You can always say it later. Sometimes, if you say too much too quickly, it's gone. You think you'll never forget it, and five minutes later you can't remember what it was. So it's better not to say it.

So that was a very big step for me in learning how to have courage in what I believed and what I saw.

For a very long time, at the weekend workshops, I was very hesitant to say anything. As Gene talked, I would think, "How can I add anything? I don't think I'm in that category. I'm not a student at university. I'm not anything." I would wait. I was certain that other people would notice some of the same things that were bothering me. Surely, somebody would say something. And they didn't!

I would wait and wait till I could no longer stand it; and then I would jump in and say something. Gene never seemed to mind. He always felt comfortable, and said, "You have never said anything wrong, and could never say anything wrong." It was all fine with him.

One time he was doing dream work, and it was the strangest dream, because in the dream, half of the dreamer's face was hard and rigid, and the other half was totally different. And as Gene worked on the dream he never said anything about that. When he was completing the dream, he asked if there were any questions. "Oh, I have a question" I said, thinking he must have known why he didn't say anything about the two halves. So I would just mention it: "How come you …?" – "Oh she's right", he said, "I didn't notice." That was always Gene: it never bothered him.

He wasn't just unbothered, but he was so quick to pick up what you were going to say.

Yes.

If you were going to pick one thing that had meaning for you inside yourself – what would come?

There was a very special man named Jay... He first came for a weeklong. I didn't happen to work with him during the week, but at the end people could sign up for a half hour with any trainer. Mostly they were people that I knew, that I had worked with. And Jay's name was on the list, but I didn't know why, because he didn't know me and I didn't know him. So he sits down and he says, with a kind of weariness: "I guess if I want help, I'm going to have to tell the story again." And I say, "No. You don't need to tell the story. You know the story. I don't need the story." "Oh, really...!"

So then I ask him, if he remembers, can sense about whatever that is…and could he just spend some time there <u>with</u> it. And suddenly he gasps, as I have never before or since heard anyone gasp: "Aaahhhhhh!" he said, "It's on my side! It's not the enemy!!" I never asked him what he was referring to, and I never needed to know. Twice he gasped like that. It took his breath away, literally.

When the weeklong was over, he came to say goodbye. He said, "You don't know this, but I'm saying goodbye to you in a new voice." So of course, that made him very special to me. I still didn't know him that well. Then he came to the four-week program, the first summer school, and I was there – helping out each week. And that's when we got to know each other better.

Then, one time, when I couldn't attend a presentation about dreams I told him I was very interested in finding out what happened in the workshop, and would he tell me about it. So we made a date. We'd go out to brunch, and he would tell me all about what happened with the dream work. He did, and we became very good friends.

And then, you went to stay with him a few times, didn't you?

Yes, he invited me to come. He had a lovely place in North Carolina – it was gorgeous there. He wanted me to teach Focusing. He would get all the people for me to teach. Everything was so comfortable and so lovely – I loved that house – and he wouldn't accept my wanting to just teach for him – no, he insisted on paying me – I would have been happy to do it for him for free – just for the visit and for being there and enjoying so much, but no...

He was really somebody very special. Sadly, he died. And when he did, he left me a sizable amount of money that I now use as scholarship money. I figure it's there to allow people to come for what they can't afford. It was a special experience that I had with him, that first time; and (tenderly) we became good friends.

Then...I remember...there was a man who had a dream that was maybe fourteen years old. Gene always says it's better to work with a fresh dream, but it was this old one that he wanted to work on. He told me that his father wasn't comfortable with feelings. There was no talk about feelings in his family. His father very much wanted him to go to school or to college, to get this education. Yet in the dream, his father didn't come to his graduation, and he had intense feelings about that – he couldn't understand why his father wouldn't come, when his father so much wanted him to study.

But I knew why his father would not come. How did I know? Because (in effect) he had just told me. I wasn't using psychological knowledge. I was just noticing what he had said. So I reminded him of what he had told me: "Maybe it was because he was afraid of what his feelings might be when you graduate" – "Ah-ahhh!" he said, "Now it makes sense." He has put two and two together. His father's fear of feelings, and his father's refusal to go where he would be overcome by feelings: of course they fit together. He said, "I never could make sense before. Now it makes sense." And I always remember that. (Bebe is speaking very softly.) Yeah...

This point about making sense is something I learned from Ray Purdy. We were having breakfast in Madison, Wisconsin; and I was telling him that Gene says, "You can't take away the parent. You can't say the parent was not good, because it's like taking away the parent, and you can't do that. It's too upsetting for the person."

And Ray said, "No, I don't think that's what it is. I think there is a need from the beginning to make sense. And if someone is supposed to take care of you when you're little, and they don't treat you right, that doesn't make sense; but if you're naughty, and they mistreat you, Oh! Then it can make sense."

So there was this strong need to make sense: and when he

said that, I said (with an edge of tears): "Let's get out of here."
I paid the bill, I got in the car, and then I sobbed my heart out.
For some reason that went so deep.

*(Slowly and softly – we are both deeply moved) You need to
make sense. The child must be able to make sense.*

Yes. The alternative is to go crazy. That's why children
blame themselves when something isn't right in their
upbringing. See. It's the only thing that can make sense. When
Daddy leaves the family: "Well, it must be something I did. It's
the only way it makes any sense." And I kept hearing people
saying, as I did with that dream, "Oh, now it makes sense." It
verified what Ray said to me: that people need to make sense.

*And that made a big shift for you – Yes, yes, yes – in your
being, in your feelings, in the moment of all that, all those tears
in the car.*

Yes – and it taught me something that has always
stayed with me: Inwardly, it needs to make sense...

So... Oh Rob, there are so many stories... I can go on and
on like this. I would probably be very embarrassed if I had to
hear all this played back.

*(Teasing) And I was going to give you the tape... (Now we are
both laughing) –* Don't you d-

*You can read it in the Folio! So tell me more... who else was
important? Gene of course was important – and I guess Mary
McGuire?*

Oh, yes. Mary was very important. There was a point when
Gene no longer wanted to do weekend workshops, so Mary
was running them, and I was still assisting. And she would
often say, "Oh, I forgot to ask you ahead of time: will you
demonstrate with me before the group?" – "Yeah, I don't mind.

Sure..." I said.

So then, she'd start with: "Where are you? – What do you want to say?"

One time I remember thinking, "Oh, my God! What if I don't have anything to say? What will I do? What if I don't come up with something?" I was feeling very nervous, and I said to her, "I'm feeling uneasy. What if I don't come up with something?"

And she said (gently): "You don't have to come up with anything. You don't need to come up with anything to get attention." Well, that was it. I wanted to just sob then. I knew we were demonstrating. I didn't feel that was the place for it. But I just wanted to cry my heart out. (Now Bebe is in tears.)

You don't have to do anything to get attention – that touches a very deep place.

Yes, see... (very tenderly, murmuring) a very deep place... Then there came the time when Mary said, "Would you want to do the Level One?" – "Sure. That's fine with me." And she said, "Well, there are only three people this time." And I said, "What difference does it make? What do I care how many there are?" – because I just loved working with the people. So I would do the Level One, and then it became the Level Two that I took on. So I used to do Level One and Two for them. (With great happiness) And it was the best part of my life, that I had all these wonderful people from all over the world...

It was the best part of your life.

(Bebe's voice is soft and intimate.) Yes... And I made friends... without having to travel. And there was...... the opportunity was like a gift, that they gave me...

(Very softly) – It was a gift that they gave you.

Yes...

Mary McGuire told a story. Mary loved her cats, and one cat died, and it was like a child to her. She was beside herself. So she called Gene to tell him what had happened. And he actually re-scheduled his class with his students at the university, to come and be with her... (Now Bebe is a little tearful once more.) I never forgot that... yeah... that's what he did...

Gene Gendlin rescheduled his class because the cat died.

Yes, he did – because he knew how much she needed his support. And so he came over there to be with her. He is such a wonderful person... I remember the day when somebody at a workshop asked him, "How do you avoid being a guru?" Because he is <u>not</u> a guru, could never be a guru. And he said, "A little honesty goes a long way." That's Gene. He is so honest about himself – he never has to hide.

And then there is a story I love to tell about partnerships. This couple had a practice together in some sort of therapy, and she came alone to the workshop. She just loved it, so then she brought her husband. They said that was the best thing that had ever happened to the two of them – Focusing together.

Gene said, "If you know these people, you know they are special people. However, if you want to try Focusing with your husband, wife, or significant other, OK. But also be sure to get another Focusing partner. You don't need one more thing your partner can't do for you!"

Previously they had only been to some other training that some man had developed which got to be very well known – with a lot of pressure on people to bring their friends. It got to be called the Forum, but it was called something different then – and it had all kinds of rules: you don't wear a watch; you don't go to the bathroom until they say you can. And so she's sitting here waiting for the rules (laughing), at a Focusing workshop. We don't have rules! – but she was thinking there <u>have</u> to be rules. We're sitting and talking, she and I, and Gene wasn't really close by. We're sitting at a break, and they always had the nuts and raisins, so she was nibbling nuts and raisins and she dropped one on the floor. I said, "That's the rule. We're not allowed to drop them on the floor!" And Gene gets up there, and he says, "EST!" I couldn't believe he heard what we were saying. (Bebe is laughing again.) Oh, he was so sharp, you know.

You hadn't seen a lot of Gene since he left Chicago...

No, I hadn't, and I missed seeing him. Then, I had an opportunity to go to New York to the theatre. I had never done that. But my son said to me, "Mother, come to New York. It is worth it." And then I realised that the only thing that would make it worth it to me was if I could see Gene.

So I called him up and I said, "I'm coming to New York. Can I see you?" – "Oh, of course!" – "When?"– "Any time!" When I got into the city, I took a taxi to his place – I was so excited – and I sat with him and we just visited. We spent about two hours together. And at one point, I said, "Did you pay attention to that?" – and he said, "You're trying to get me to focus!" We had such a wonderful visit

And then, a few days later there was a message from Gene. Gene never calls. <u>Never</u>. If I call and he's busy, he says, "Call later." He doesn't call back. But this time there was a message from Gene. He said, "When you left, I realised how much you brought loving – so thank you." (Bebe is crying now...)

That touches you very deeply.

(Tenderly) – You know that's the way he says goodbye... he doesn't say goodbye, he says, "So hello!" – and that was the end of the message. And I told him I would cherish it forever.

(Softly) It meant a great deal to you, and it still does...it still does. You brought him so much loving.

(With much feeling...) Yes. Thank you. Coming from him that was unbelievable. He picked up the phone to call me...

The other thing that I'm remembering was when I was given a surprise party for my 70th birthday, and Atsmaout's husband took the pictures for my birthday – and there were pictures of Gene blowing up the balloons – and I think it was Reva who saw the pictures and said, "He never blew any balloons up for me!"

OK. Maybe that's a good place to stop.

Probably.

Let's see. Is there any last thing that feels important about Bebe and Gene and Focusing?

One time I asked him to listen to me because I had a problem with sleeping and I could not get any resolution for it. And he did. He listened to me and I wanted to pay him and he wouldn't let me. He said, "You have helped so much." So I said, "Then I cannot ask you again if you will not take money for this session that I had with you." I remember that. He would not let me pay him...Yep...

A wise and a kind and a generous man – and one whom you're very much involved with in your feelings and your life... However, the biggest feeling, when we were talking, was Ray Purdy saying to you, "It needs to make sense." Maybe one of the two or three great revelatory moments for you...

Yes. It needs to make sense. There is a need, a basic need to make sense...

A basic need...

It went in so deep and so fast. I just sobbed my heart out. (With much feeling) – I don't know why it hit me that hard, but it did.

It absolutely touched the child in you, who could not make sense, and who tied herself in knots to make sense –

(Softly) – Maybe.

– of what was crazy-making

– Maybe.

Something like that.

It could be, but I have little memory of my childhood.

But something knows, or the tears wouldn't come.

Yes...

And I wish I could tell <u>you</u> something, but I don't know if it's necessarily for this...

(Rob is laughing, but Bebe is serious) – So shall I stop the tape?

Yes.

A MEETING PLACE

for my friend Bebe Simon
most sensitive of observers
most intuitive of guides
most loving of friends
who stood in a doorway
and asked me in

how does the whole of this-

this problem
this issue
this relationship
this project
this forming poem
or painting
or music
this dream
or memory
or fantasy
this grief
this happiness
this cage
this liberty

-how does the whole of this feel in my body?
…in the middle of my body?

this is the felt sense
within myself

I   touching my felt sense

'you want me to touch this?-
this vagueness?
this unclear? unsatisfactory? insubstantian
global fuzzy and furry?
-this .... ?' 'Yeah, this ....'

sensing its connection with something in my life:

what is its quality?
what is its form?
what words come there?
what sounds and images grow there?
when I dig around this boulder, does it rock?
what is its nature?
what is its worst?
what is my direction?

if the tide threatens to overwhelm me
can I reach dry land?
if explanation, analysis and blind thinking interrupt me
can I mildly murmur 'thankyou and no thankyou'?
if I begin to attack myself, acid/alkali corrosive, to sink or

beat
myself up
    can I say 'yeah - that's good cement: you can dump it
over there
    right here I've got this little green shoot
    and I mean to protect it! '?

oh yeah - touching and sensing, listening and waiting
    so gently
    so very gently
    where whatever comes is welcome like fresh air
    even when it is grief-stricken or forbidden
    bitter or violent
    particularly when it is grief-stricken or forbidden
    bitter or violent
    guilty, sexual, embarrassed
    raging, hateful ....

potato plants
in a dark cellar
grow deformed
and I too
need sun and rain and wind and weather
strong roots and black soil -
what soil? what weather? what ground? what tending?

....listening.....

if it wanted to open in some way
    would I be open to that opening?

if it wanted to speak to me in some way
      would I be deaf or hearing?
if it wanted ....
.... would I welcome that?
how does the whole of this feel in my body? ....
in the middle of my body?

II   touching my felt sense
how does my body want to be?
      to sit or lie
      to crawl or curl up
      to stand or move
      to express me
      in growl or purr or scratch or snuggle?
what language of my soul
      is written in my flesh? in muscle and sinew
      in tension or in action?

what dream or fantasy is caught here
      like the frog in a fairy tale
      trapped and waiting
      all these passing years
      for the prince's kiss?
where is this mute-wise body trying to lead me?
      what regression?
      what catharsis?

a step comes
a change of energy

a ripple of movement sweeps
the constellations of my heavens-
      where the lights went out so long ago....
      .... I had not thought to see them lit again....
radiating, echoing, repatterning
      my myth, my now, my expectation -
a shimmering wave pervades my seeming chaos
my infinite, intricate, interdependent, irregular fractal geom-
etries -wind of change blows rain and flowers
      n deserts of my soul....

can I now receive this gift
      ope, wonderment
these tears of transformation
this release?

and between us

III   touching....

how shall I express myself to you
      n words
      n tune, as the healer called it:
      don't listen to the words: listen to the tune!'
      in gesture -
      he language of my body
      eey, hand and skin

how shall I express myself to you?

IV   touching....

how do I want you to respond to me?
- with eye contact, poised awareness and silent attention?
- with neat deft precis of my words?
- with sensitive ear for hidden sense and feeling?
- with close 'intuitive attention (whilst I am silent)
to my subtle bodily indications?
I listen to your tune and gesture
- your honesty, openness and real presence here
- your tentative suggestions, guiding, leading and following
- your skill and special knowledge of ways to bring healing
- I sense how I need you to be, and I tell you
and yet there is more! listen to me, there is more!

V   touching....
       touching....

how do I need to express myself to you
          in my touching you
in my holding
stroking
tickling
resisting
fighting you?
in my moving and dancing with you?
play of laughter
clutch of terror
song or drum?

VI   touching my felt sense

how do I invite you to be with me
        in your touching me?

and so ....
        ....I turn inside
        wait and listen
        trust and am gentle

touching....

living
        breathing
        experiencing

here
now
in the eternal present

keeping company
in your company
with myself ....

Rob Foxcroft
12 December 1989
meditativelistening@gmail.com

PREVIOUSLY UNPUBLISHED
WRITINGS

ANOTHER VIEW OF "YES, BUT"

Previously unpublished article

"YES, BUT" MAY NOT always be a game. It may instead be a cry to be heard, that would best be answered through the use of active listening, at the same time achieving the other person's goal to be helpful.

It has been generally understand in the TA model that when suggestions for improving a distressful situation in someone's life are responded to with "Yes, But," a game is being played or at least attempted.

The person making the suggestion may feel unappreciated in their sincere efforts to be helpful. They may also feel irritated and believe that the complainer does not really wish to make changes. A professional listener may include that a problem does exist and may feel that treatment is in order.

If the person speaking of a troublesome area in their life, experiences a feeling of confusion following being accused of playing "Yes, But," a different view may be more accurate. As Claude Steiner pointed out (Steiner, 1974), a feeling of confusion follows a discount. In this case, the discount is of the cry to be heard that goes unanswered, the seeking for empathy that the complaining represents. In many instances, the "Yes, But" is the polite attempt to acknowledge the helpful responses that are not fitting the need. In addition, the helpful suggestions also discount whatever thought, time, and effort the complainer may have already spent in attempting to resolve the problem.

If, instead, the complainer could be aware of, and willing to risk expressing their true need, they might then say that they are not feeling heard, that suggestions are not what they want at the time, and they would really appreciate it if the other person would just listen to them.

A sincere effort to be helpful or therapeutic would best be achieved by active listening (Gendlin, 1981). This would require asking the speaker to repeat what was said, and reflecting it back until the speaker feels heard. And having felt heard, enables the speaker to move toward resolution at their own pace, and circumvents any need for "Yes, But."

References
Gendlin, E. *Focusing*. NY: Bantam Books, 1981.
Steiner, C. *Scripts People Live*. NY: Grove Press, 1974.

A METHOD OF FOCUSING FOR SELF-EMPATHY IN STRESSFUL SITUATION

Previously unpublished article about "crossing" NVC and Focusing

IN ATTEMPTING TO USE a method of nonviolent communication I inadvertently combined it with Focusing and discovered a new way to facilitate a shift. I also found I was listening to myself empathetically in a stressful situation when no one was readily available to listen to me. Excited about my discovery I have used it repeatedly. It has extended to using it with other people, often on the phone, and some who don't know Focusing or the method of nonviolent communication.

First let me share with you briefly something about the nonviolent communication method and then I want to tell you how it all came about.

Marshall Rosenberg's Model for Nonviolent Communication (see footnote below) includes: expressing what I am observing or recalling in action language; stating how I am feeling about it and my values or experience that gave birth to the feeling; making a request for nurturance in positive action language. These statements serve to share one's vulnerability, which may inspire compassionate response, and often results in receiving the nurturance requested.

To illustrate: first expressing or recalling what I am observing in action language, "When you were late . . . "; then stating how I felt about it, "I felt furious and helpless,"; and owning my values or experience that gave birth to the feelings, ". . . because I experience that as not being able to depend on what you say to me."; finally making a request for nurturance in positive action language, "I would like you to say back to me what I just said so I know you heard me."

The model also includes empathetically receiving the same truth from others. On this point Marshall Rosenberg frequently states a person can only give empathy to others if one has some resources for receiving some as well. And now through Focusing I could be my own resource when necessary. Here is how I came upon this awareness.

Usually when I feel angry I choose not to communicate it. I assume I understand the other person's situation, which negates my right to be angry. Or I anticipate a negative response if I were to tell them how I feel. Saying nothing leaves me feeling my hurt and wanting to distance myself from the person who was so "thoughtless". In such a situation I decided to try the model for nonviolent communication. However, I found I was not in touch with either how I really felt, how I experienced the situation, or what I wanted.

My friend had been late. I was angry and tempted to attack critically. Instead I said nothing. He didn't notice my silence, which fed my rage. Then I had a long wait alone in the car while he went to get our next passenger. I was in no mood to enjoy where we were going. So I decided to express myself according to the model, and found myself stuck just thinking about what to say. So I took the questions inside to find out what was I really feeling about the situation. I waited and wondered and kept asking, "What was I feeling?" When something came to me, I checked to see if it was really right. When I knew it fit the body sense, I went on to ask again, "How was I experiencing that situation?" and waited. When the response came, I felt a shift, was no longer angry and was looking forward to our outing. Now I only wanted to share the wonder I felt about what I had just experienced. It was then I realized I had used the nonviolent communication model in what felt like a natural way to facilitate my Focusing. I was aware that in times of stress or conflict the felt sense of the whole situation is very strong, is clearly in my body, though very unclear as to what it is all about. Now I had a quick way to find out when I needed it most.

The next time I used the method I was upset about my Focusing partner signing up for a class on the night we had planned to have the Changes group. There seemed to be no convenient alternative. When I asked the question, "What I feel is ____?" and waited, I was looking for the quality of the felt sense, the handle. The first things that popped into my head, frustration, anger, I recognized as the old familiar labels that kept me from looking with fresh curiosity for what was in it this time. I continued to ask and wait, checking each word or image, resonating them with the felt sense to see if they were really right. When the answer came . . . "Alone" . . . , there was not doubt about the fit or rightness of it. "Yes, I felt alone with what I was wanting." Then the next question, "because I experience that as . . ." and waiting. Quickly I knew,

"Because if I am the only one with that want, I have no chance of getting it, because I don't count." That connected to my needing to sell everything I like to others. I just had to find someone else to want what I did! Though the urgency beneath that selling usually defeated my goal. "WOW" If that was how I experienced the situation, no wonder I felt the way I did!

I find myself thinking about this new method when talking with friends. They mention a particularly upsetting incident, or task yet to be done. I hear that it grabs them in the body just thinking about it, and I check that out. Then instead of wondering what to say or offering advice I suggest trying something else. If they are willing, I have them ask and wait as I had done. When it works, frequently, the short amount of time to get the body sense to open and speak to them, and the depth they sometimes reach amazes me. If the incident has already passed and recalling it grabs them freshly, it works as well.

Are you willing to try it for yourself and see?

How new Method compares with Focusing Steps

1. Clear a Space .. Conflict or stressful situation fills body with felt sense, seeming

2. Felt Sense . . . . . to have cleared all else out.

3. Handle . . . . .Asking, what I feel and wait for quality of felt sense.

4. Resonate . . . . . . Check what comes against felt sense.

5. Ask . . . . .Because I experience that as . . . . ?

6. Receive . . . . . . .Protect, be glad it spoke, know how it came.

7. Is it okay to stop here . . . . If needed, next step, Ask what I want and wait.

_____

_____

The original text included this footnote: 1. <u>Model for Nonviolent Communication</u>, Marshall B. Rosenberg, PhD. For copies of book, or more information, Center for Nonviolent Communication, 3229 Bordeaux, Sherman TX 75090.

BEBE, THE STORYTELLER, WITH FOCUSING TALES OF WONDERMENT

Transcribed from a recording of an oral presentation that Bebe gave at the International Focusing Conference in 1991

I WANT TO TELL THE STORY just as it happened, so you can reexperience it with me. Hopefully it may inspire you to tell stories of your own that will fit the purpose of this presentation.

Now some background before I begin. This man was interested in learning Focusing. He knew about it from his wife who had been Focusing regularly with the same partner for many years. She asked me if I would give him lessons. I asked for a six session commitment by which time we could judge together if he needed more or not. I had never seen him. He called and we set up an appointment after discussing the details.

The day he arrived was a warm summer day and he obviously was a runner, in shorts and running shoes, with beautiful well-developed calf muscles, and he was tan and tall and strong looking, a fairly young man. Of course, such things are relative. He was a teacher.

I began finding I would not need as much introduction as I usually would since he did seem to have some idea of what I meant by Focusing. I was going to find out whether he would be able to clear a space. I wanted to get a feeling for how well he would pick up the process. He very quickly got confused. When I would suggest things like can you set something out? He would say he doesn't know what that means, or that it is him, so how can he put it down. Of course you know, and I hasten to reassure, you, all of this was done bit by bit, and interspersed with my saying "If it doesn't feel right, don't do it."

As I suggested gently that he go inside and be with what was there, he began to tremble, visibly shaking. That I had never experienced before, and it frightened me. What was I getting into? I am not a therapist and had never had anyone with such a reaction to gentle focusing ideas.

I was even more careful then to check that he wasn't interpreting my words from his past experience. He at some point told me that a therapist told him that the only way to overcome his problem was just to go in and come out the other side. He tried to do that and ended up in the hospital and it took 7 days to come out; so any words that said "go in" scared him. I then very carefully clarified that I did not know what he needed and only his inner wisdom can guide both of us. He got the idea that he had his own power and that felt good. The shaking stopped and when the session was over and he left, I looked out the window as he walked out of the building and down the street to see him jumping for joy with his hand going up in the air and I felt good about making a good start.

At the next visit, he saw himself carrying a heavy bucket of tar or some kind of unwanted messy stuff and it had a lid on it.

I told him it was only up to him if he was curious and wanted to lift the lid and peek inside. That was firm "no"! But he got the power to decide whether or not to look and he could even set it down if he was tired of carrying the weight. That was a new idea that pleased him, of having total control.

When we got around to the idea of the little boy inside who might need company and would he see a way to sit with him, maybe on a park bench or whatever he would like to do. "No, but if I bend down on one knee, then I can look straight at him and that's alright." That is one I have never thought or heard of before. So he visualized being down in front of the little boy talking to him, and then he said, "He asked if he could hug me". He told me he was not very comfortable with hugging so he was glad the little boy had asked first, and it felt alright to let him do that. It felt very good to have this contact with the little boy. He was surprised to find that he could relate to the little boy on this level. He said again how happy he was that the little boy has asked him first and not just hugged him.

Again there is none of this that I would have thought to suggest. I'm not taking credit for what happened, except that I was just being with him very, very gently, very carefully, and following his lead.

It turned out, as it happened, and now we will get into the interesting story of what was going on in his life. He was one of two sons and a daughter, and he was his mother's favorite. To the extent that, even though there was always a father in the picture, and they were still married and together, he was taking his father's place, and she knew it and my client knew it, and the whole world knew it. When he had talked to her about this later in life, all she was sorry about was that everybody had to know it, not what she had done.

His mother was very ill, had been on dialysis for years, and he had recently helped her to decide to stop the treatments and to die. The doctors said it might take 3 days for the poison in her system to kill her. So he was spending most of his time at her side, in a hospital at the other side of the city, except for traveling back and forth to spend a couple of hours with his little children. He wanted to be there with his mother, holding her hand when she died, because he was everything to her and she was everything to him.

He imagined then that he was bending over and he saw his mother in her hospital bed and suddenly he got this image, like a little tiny figure, maybe sort of a butterfly, rising from her bed coming over to meet the little speck and how good that felt as they met. Then he saw somebody or more than one person covering the body with lots and lots of sheets, many layers, and he knew that though he would be sad without her, he didn't need the body anymore and he could let it go. These two tiny little figures were happy to be together and it felt right. The end of the story is that night she died.

All I want to say about that is if I were the most creative person in the whole world and the most brilliant, I could not have come up with one of those images, not one. He made an appointment for another session after I returned, but while I was away he decided he needed a therapist who would be more directive and who knew Focusing and he had found one. I hadn't seen him, but heard from his wife about when his mother died.

The point of the story is I believe that following the person's inner place is far beyond anything anybody could come up with.

I saw him once after that to ask his permission to tell his story.

So with that I want to give you time to ask anything, say anything.

Stephen Feher spoke up and said he was touched by the way I was able to be with him. "My experience with you is you are so present and very unobtrusive and kind, and I'm sure it was a very great gift you gave him". I said thank you, and acknowledged that he did say something about my contribution the last time we spoke.

Shortly after the end of his sessions I heard about a book called "Emotional Incest" and told his wife and they bought is and she told me it was a perfect fit. At the time I was working with him I wasn't thinking in those terms or anything like that. He is still a long way from healed from all the pain that is now first coming to light. If she was still alive I don't know if he would have touched it.

But I did want to share with you that to me what come out of that inner place with the Focusing process never ceases to be a wonderment.

Luke Lukens said next, that though he couldn't remember the exact words I had said something like 'I didn't do anything, all I did was pay attention to him and follow him', but to me that's everything, that is everything."

I said, "Yes, I guess so, and I did stay close and encourage him to be gentle and all the things we know about, like take your time, just wait there, something is there, what is that?, all that kind of things. It was simple guiding, I wasn't bringing in anything else that I knew about.

Ton Coffeng asked for clarification about the beginning when the client was shaking. I said again about how it was most of the first visit, but that at the end, when we talked, I has assured the client that I had no agenda for him about what he needed to do, that was not what I was there for. The second time he came back was when I went even slower and smaller steps and was then he made the huge step to the bucket of tar.

Ton went on then, "I recognize you respected his shaking and your own feeling of helplessness there. I share with you my own experience. It was at one of the Focusing workshops and I was Focusing very deeply with M.G. and all of a sudden I got very deeply hit by the war (and we won the war) and I don't know where it came from, and my friends didn't know what to do and just left me there lying on the ground. Last year I went to a therapist and he told me that this shaky business "I don't know if you can ever come out of that." (Laughter drowns Ton's last words about the therapist and additional few words.) I said sarcastically, "So you'd be stuck forever, that's great."

Then Ton referred to the work of Gary Prouty who follows and some great thing may happen. But in really traumatized clients who are suffering a great deal and don't seen able to get small steps or to slow them down, then he, Ton, can't stand to see them suffer so much. He asked about my experience in such cases. I told him I hadn't dealt with any people like that so I couldn't say.

But I clarified that what I had done was not slow my client down as much as slowing myself down and when I said anything to him I asked him to repeat what I has said so I kept us close together that way, to make sure he had heard me and not gone off on something he thought I said.

"I don't know with people like you are referring to, what would work." But this same young man later came close to being hospitalized more recently and his wife called for his therapist who came to the house. But before the therapist got there, and in spite of the fact that her husband doesn't usually like this reflecting, it bothers him when she does it, that night the only thing that worked was when she repeated only what he said. That was all he could respond to. So I thought that was very interesting, that when he was in a desperate condition, that's when he responded to, her reflecting his words, even though he didn't most of the time. With me he had no trouble with being listened to. Luke said "I don't know the other person, but you have a quality that people perceive you as really being with them, not just saying something.

Of course I said the other is his wife and maybe when she does it with other people it is different. I don't know that, it's hard to say, not being there. But there was no way I could know that first time, to be forewarned that he had that terrible experience so that anything said to him about that little place inside was terror. I don't take histories and I don't know if it would have come out anyway. But it didn't matter, it turned out it was really the only thing I could have offered.

Luke: "it makes me think of one thing as far as being a guide is concerned.... I had an experience with a guy, it went very well and everything, but afterward he said when you said my words back, word for word, I didn't feel met. This was a couple of weeks or a month ago. I wish he had told me that during the session, but I need to find more effective ways to tell people that I want you to tell me that when it comes up and not afterwards."

I told Luke that is why I say that only talking afterwards, especially after the first session, sometimes more than the first couple of times, do you learn what you need to know. They don't know what to say in the middle, and it's all so new and you're new, and you don't know their process, so it does take some time to find the right balance of what they need, how you can come out to meet them.

Ian Yomans: "it's like dancing with anybody for the first time on the floor, just positioning the foot."

"Not stepping on each others toes." (cant' recognize whose voice)

"Exactly. It's not about Focusing, you are talking about our eternal process. I went to see somebody just before I left England 3 years ago. I hadn't seen him in 30 years, and doing that funny little dance around people you haven't seen for a long time, I just thought to myself, Ken, I know you used to limp, but you used to limp with your other leg. So over lunch it got raised and he said, "Yes, I had a very bad accident, a car smash, on the other side so it took me to limp on this other one. A much bigger one, in fact I nearly lost my leg." It was very interesting, Ian went on, "He's a pharmacist so he had some medical knowledge." He said to me, "It was strange, I nearly lost a leg, but they did a very good job they saved it for me. But there was one very curious thing happened during the whole of the initial emergency treatment which was that I came out of my coma to see myself looking at the blood bag, and I said, and I can remember hearing, being astonished at how powerful my voice was, "You've got the wrong group, and then delineated the group and I didn't wait for an answer, I just went back into my coma. When I came out I carry this card that says I've got these interesting antibodies."

(At that point the tape runs out.)

There were more comments but nothing was said about any more stories that would come under the heading of Focusing tales of wonderment. Rather more about strange experiences people had that were not related to Focusing.

BEBE'S THOUGHTS ON GUIDING (SHORTER VERSION)

Previously unpublished article

AS I THINK OF ORGANIZING what there is for me to say about my way of guiding, I am aware of two primary areas to be covered. The attitude of guiding comes first because it underlies all else. It is something on which I believe we can all agree, that of "being with". Secondarily, there is language awareness, which includes both the language used by the guide and that of the Focuser.

First though, a word about styles of guiding. Notice the use of my name in the title, which is to say that it is only *my* way, and not that of all guides. Notice also the use of the plural, styles, which says that there are many, and they are very individual. I believe each of us incorporates that which we find comfortable and also useful, which adds up to that which feels right. Style cannot be taught. It may be much like the budding artist, who begins by emulating those they admire until they find themselves. There are, however, some basics around which you build your style: attitude and language awareness.

First and foremost is the attitude of "being with" another person in their Focusing process. "Being with" requires full attention and trusting the process. The purpose of "being with" is to enable the Focuser to pay attention in the center of their body so as to be guided by their own process. Therefore, the first few minutes need to be for letting the Focuser's attention turn inward.

I encourage the Focuser to begin by taking a few centering steps: a couple of deep breaths to help quiet their thinking mind and bring their attention into their body, so they are ready to notice how they are in the present moment. A couple of minutes to be aware of their physical body and the space it is occupying, what they may be touching, and then, just the air around them.

In enabling the focuser to become aware of what is there, you, the guide, must transmit your attitude of the importance of paying attention to slight body senses that could be easily overlooked. There is often a tendency, particularly in new focusers, to be selective in noticing only those things that they think are appropriate. You may suspect this picking and choosing is taking place during a very long silence. It is then helpful to check it out by asking what is happening so you can be with them.

Here a note that there are times, with some people, when it is necessary to attend to the signals in the peripheral areas, such as head, shoulders, arms, or legs, for example. These may be instead of, or in addition to, what is in the body. If there are only these outer senses and nothing in the center, the guide might suggest to the focuser to see what it would be like in the center *if* these senses were taken inside. If neither of these feel right to the focuser (the inside place may not yet feel ready to reveal itself), it has worked to focus on those outer senses in the same way as on a felt sense, though always alert to some slight stirring inside.

A necessary ingredient, if this attention to even slight body senses is to be learned by the focuser, is for you to encourage them to take their time. Many, perhaps most focusers have a tendency to hurry themselves along in the process as they do in other areas of their lives. When the inside place feels rushed it may just close down, leaving a note, "gone for the day". So your attitude of being patient if it doesn't happen quickly that they can go inside and find what is there, and all along the way as well, is critical. Even when their process does move very quickly from one thing to anothers, it is helpful to suggest that they slow down and allow their body to rest at each step.

At the same time, the attitude of "being with" must include your encouraging the focuser to take a friendly attitude toward whatever is there and whatever comes. That does not imply liking what they find or accepting what comes. For the idea of accepting often carries an implied should. When the inside place hears it should accept something it often refuses to cooperate, may say a firm no, or again worst of all, it shuts down. On the other hand, what is important is enabling them to just acknowledge it.

Enabling the focuser to acknowledge what is there and taking time to just be with it in a friendly way helps It to feel safe. Only when It feels safe, believes "It" is really being listened to, and not pushed to do anything, will "It" be ready to speak. So as the guide it is vital to know you are not there to fix it, and you are there to enable them to learn also to just be with "It" without trying to fix it.

The attitude of "being with" is demonstrated by your gentle

tone of voice and by offering only suggestions in a tentative manner, and no commands. This tells them your suggestions are only to be tried if it feels right to do so at the time. This carries the message that you are ready to hear whatever their response may be, yes, or no, to your suggestions. It says you have no ego investment in anything you say and are ready to drop it if it doesn't fit. In other words, you are showing them that you trust their process to guide both of you, enabling them to do the same. When they can believe inside that "no" is as welcome as "yes" in response to your suggestion, they will begin to be able to allow whatever is there.

Here it is necessary to mention the need for you to notice if the person shakes their head "no", they could mean two very different things. The "no" that says the suggestion doesn't fit is one. Then you tell them to just let it go without giving it any undue attention. The other "no" is the place inside saying it doesn't feel right or doesn't want to follow the suggestion. Your readiness to step back and be with the place that says no, it doesn't want to, may be critical. Encouraging the person to take time with this place and follow where "it" may lead will feel right to them. In my experience, however, one of the most difficult aspects of guiding has been enabling the new focuser to allow the inside place to say "no". The inclination seems to be to regard the guide as an expert whose suggestions should be tried at all cost. Instead, here we come to asking inside. First of all, would it be right to ask a question at all?

BEBE'S THOUGHTS ON GUIDING (LONGER VERSION)

Previously unpublished article

I ORGANIZE MY THOUGHTS about the way I guide around two primary areas, attitude and language awareness. The attitude of guiding is primary because it underlies all else. Secondarily, the guide must be aware of both his/her own use of language, as well as that of the Focuser.

But first, just a word about styles of guiding. I call your attention to the use of my name in the title. That is done to tell you that it is only *my* way, and not that of all guides. Notice also that I say styles, which says there are many. I find them to be quite individual. I believe we each incorporate that which we find comfortable and useful, which adds up to that which feels right. Style cannot be taught. It may be likened to the budding artist, who at first, and perhaps for a long time, emulates those they admire, until they find themselves. Their work reflects this change. However, you do build your style around the basics; attitude and language.

First and foremost is the attitude of "being with" another person in their Focusing process. "Being with" requires full attention to, as well as trusting in, the inner process of the

Focuser. The purpose of "being with" is to enable the Focuser to pay attention in the center of their body, so as to direct both the guide and themselves along the path of that inner process.

Therefore, the first few minutes need to be for letting the Focuser's attention turn inward. The amount of time needed for this will vary according to the person's own natural pace as well as whether or not they have had any experience with paying attention to that place in themselves. If not, they may need help to learn this.

I begin by suggesting that the Focuser just be aware of their physical body and the space it occupies. This is to help quiet their thinking mind so they are ready to notice how they are in their body at the present moment. I might say, "Notice where you are touching something, where the chair is holding you, where your feet are touching the floor, the differences in texture, hard or soft, rough or smooth, that you might notice where your hands or arms are touching. Also notice where nothing is touching, and there is only the air around you."

Next I suggest they take a couple of deep breaths. "Notice when you let the air all the way out, where that is happening..." and I point to that place just below the rib cage.

At the same time, I am aware that at times, or with some people, the attention of the Focuser is taken with feelings in the peripheral areas, such as the head, shoulders, arms, or legs. These may be instead of, or in addition to, what is in the center of the body. I tell them, "It is alright to acknowledge whatever you notice, wherever it is." Doing this hopefully permits them to also notice how they are inside.

"Being with" the focuser in the inside place also requires "being with" in a listening mode. Listening is an integral part of guiding. Listening to the focuser, setting the example for them to learn to listen to themselves and other people, may be the greatest gift of guiding.

I use the term listening in a broader sense of not just listening to what you hear but also to what you see. This includes noticing the emphasis on some words more than others, the facial and body expressions, the breathing of the focuser, the tearing of the eyes, the reddening of the nose or the change of color on the face, etc. Sensing when to reflect what you have seen or heard, or when to just "be with" in silence, is the goal of listening. "Being with" in silence may allow the focuser the time needed to be listening to the inside place, in order to notice whatever is there.

A very long silence, however, leads me to wonder if the novice Focuser is doing selective noticing of only the things they deem appropriate. Sometimes a furrowed brow, a pained expression suggests to me they are stuck and finding this hard work because they are picking and choosing what to notice and ignoring other things. Here the guide needs to find out what is going on, and at the same time not to disturb the process.

I use this opportunity to say that noticing what is there, does *not* automatically include telling me. I tell them, "Focusing is as private a process as you wish it to be. I only need to know about the process, not the content. So when it feels okay to do so, would you tell me where you are so I can be with you."

This brings us to the attitude of the focuser as he or she is "being with" the place inside. They will probably need the help of the guide to remember or to learn for the first time about being friendly and gentle to whatever is there. They need to be told that noticing and acknowledging what is there does not necessarily include liking what is there. I usually say something like, "You probably would know how to be with a friend who happened to be in need of some company, and not be harsh with them if they were troubled or didn't feel like saying much. Can you be with yourself in the same way, just listening and not trying to fix it."

It is equally important for the guide to be able to listen without trying to fix it, which would only intrude on the space inside. Only there, with time and attention, can "it" know what is right, when "it" feels safe to say it. Enabling the focuser to give "it" the time and feeling of being listened to, perhaps for the first time, is an important purpose in guiding. As the guide you can help the focuser to take time with each step along the way. Enabling the focuser to slow down their process, to let the body heal along the way, when there is often a tendency to rush from one thing to the next, is also significant. Here I might say, "Take your time, as much as you need, and let me know when *you* are ready to move on."

Another part of guiding that must be mentioned here is the how and when of asking questions. They are always offered as a suggestion, with no ego investment on the part of the guide. By that I mean checking if it feels right to the Focuser to ask any question at that point, and if that particular question also feels right, and if not, being ready to quickly forget the whole thing without having to distract the Focuser by their having to say why it doesn't fit. Sometimes I even offer the *idea* of asking first. I would say, "I have something to suggest. If and when it feels okay, just let me know." If they say they want to hear it, I would offer the question and then say, "If it doesn't feel right, just let it go by. Don't even answer me."

With people who are new to the process, it is necessary to be clear first that all questions are intended to be taken inside to ask and then just wait. The object of questions is not to be answered by the focuser to you, the guide, nor for them to answer themselves from what they already know. Rather, to ask and wait with the attitude of wonder and curiosity, as if they were asking someone else and really had no idea what the answer might be.

When instead, there is an immediate reply, you, the guide, need to help them notice that they did not take it inside to ask and wait. Rather, they answered off the top of their head, which didn't bring anything they didn't already know. I take such an opportunity to clarify about how such things get in the way of the process, even when trying to be helpful. Here I say something like, "You answered so quickly, that must have come from your head [as always, fully prepared to be wrong and stand corrected]. I know your head wants to be helpful, may even fear that it won't be needed anymore now that you have this new source of information. But like the judgmental thoughts that are always ready to jump in about what you are noticing, what you might just be thinking of saying, or have already said, that part, often called the critic, is not usually helpful to this process. You can tell because it isn't anything at all new. Though perhaps at times it seems quite on target, it hasn't brought the changes you are wanting. If all that was needed was thinking about the problem, which you have probably already done many times, it would already be fixed. So something else seems to be in order here, such as going inside and asking and waiting for some new direction or some fresh air, which brings with it a change in energy you can notice."

When in fact something a bit new does come, whether from just being with it, or from asking a question, then the guide helps the focuser to stop and notice what came. Also to receive and protect it, as well as to notice how it felt when it came. And to notice *how* it came, by suggesting that they retrace the steps just before it came, and to mark the place so they can get to keep it.

Often the signs that something did come are fleeting ones. If the guide fails to notice, it may also be missed by the focuser. So the kind of "listening" mentioned before is called for here. Noticing an almost smile, gone before it took hold, or the lift of the head. A widening of the eyes for a moment, a sound of slight surprise, hmmm, may be all there is at first. If I notice something like this, I then ask, "Did something just come there, and was there an unexpected quality to it?" If there is a yes here, then I say, "Notice how it felt when it came. Take time to receive it, be glad it spoke, and protect it from your head jumping on it and dumping on it with things like, 'what good is that?' or 'it doesn't make any sense', or 'what are you going to do now?' Just take time to be with it, mark the place so you can get back to it if you wish to. It might help to take a minute to retrace the steps from where you started to how you got to this place."

As the guide, I have found it most useful to notice and mention when there are signs of positive energy. Only then are they allowed to fully take hold and be welcomed. Otherwise the new focuser often assumes the seriousness of what we are doing precludes the acceptability of an ear-to-ear grin, or a desire to giggle or laugh aloud.

Also, when something comes, it is helpful for the guide to encourage the focuser to take a minute first to just be with it, to integrate it, and only then to check and see what, if anything, *it* wishes to share. I usually caution focusers to make a habit of this, even if they are with their most trusted confidant. Inside has its own ideas about sharing. The deepest places seem to be quiet ones where, at least at first, no words are needed. Even the most vocal people often come to this place where they have no need to say anything, and rather would just be there with it. Again the attitude of the guide, being comfortable with just keeping this quiet place company, enables the Focuser to do likewise. Saying, "If it feels right just to be with it for now and not say anything, just take your time."

Another part of the basic attitude of "being with" comes into play around the area of reflecting and suggestions. As the guide is being guided by the focuser's inner process, all ideas or questions are offered to "it" as suggestions, tentatively. Sometimes I ask first, "If it would feel right, try _____." If I haven't said it first, I may say it after I offer the idea. If I haven't said it at all, I try to convey it by my tone of voice. It is most important to have said it enough times before getting started, and along the way, that the Focuser feels free to follow his or her own sense of rightness above anything the guide may suggest, though seen as an expert. In keeping with this idea, I would avoid as much as possible offering anything by saying, "I want you to _____", which may be taken as a command.

Making it very clear that "yes" or "no" replies to a suggestion are equally welcome is most necessary. As a rule, I have found this to be very difficult to convey to new people. There are two kinds of "no" for the guide to consider. When it is obvious that the suggestion hasn't touched the focuser, usually seen by something like a blank expression that says, "No connection made here", then just move on, as I have said earlier regarding questions. When the Focuser's inside place says "No" with a felt sense that has, in fact, shown that something has been touched, then it is appropriate to back up to "be with" the place that says "no". Only, of course, if the Focuser confirms that "it feels right" to be with that place.

As the guide is reflecting, there is a choice of language to be considered. There are times that it is best to reflect using the Focuser's exact words. This doesn't mean necessarily using all their words. But when you are finding you don't know what to say next, it is always safe to use *their* words. Also it is most important to listen for and say back any "fire engine" words (meaning those that stand out from the rest of what is going by). Also include the emphasis of those words, sometimes even dramatizing them with added emphasis. Always you are wanting to convey by your words that you are "being with" them, and it is okay with you wherever they are.

Another way that message comes across is by your choosing simple words, that the inside place can relate to. Complex terms on the other hand, may draw them away from that place and back up to their head, or at least say to them that you are not comfortable with their place inside. There are of course exceptions, but as a rule I have found it most useful.

It is also helpful to use direct words such as "there", "that place", as you point your finger to draw attention to the inside place.

One word I would avoid without exception is "Why" and

any questions that ask why. It is always a straight line to the head. Instead I have used the 'what' approach. For instance, "If it would feel right, see what went on there just before the heavy feeling intruded in your space." At times what went on there is revealed to the guide by the language of the focuser.

Though I have mentioned the critic earlier, it is worth noting here again. Listening for any words used by the focuser that are of a judgmental nature, that sound like dumping on oneself, the guide may safely assume that they originate in the critic. Though the guide is listening for feeling words that indicate a felt sense inside, there is also a felt sense that comes from the messages of the critic, such as guilt or fear. This is especially evident where there was something light there which changed suddenly. These messages bear negative energy, and that may be what the guide notices, sometimes even before there are any words to confirm it. At such times the guide's reflections bringing it to the attention of the focuser can be most helpful, as they may have missed the cause of the change inside them. I would offer a suggestion to the focuser to pay attention to what happened. I might say, "Can you go back to notice what came in just before that heavy feeling took over?"

Significant clues to the guide can come from noticing the level of the words used by the focuser, whether of simplicity or sophistication. Words that usually come from the head include intellectual descriptions, which are not congruent with what has been coming from the inside place. These include labels such as anxiety, frustration, old familiar terms well known and not at all fresh. When labels are used they serve to keep the person from looking at what it is they are really experiencing under the guise of these terms. So here I would suggest,

"Notice what is the quality of the felt sense you are calling anxiety, frustration, etc. What is it this time, even though it seems the same as before."

Whenever the focuser uses quality words, the guide knows it signifies not only a handle for the felt sense, but more importantly, that they do in fact have a felt sense. Then reflecting the quality words helps the focuser to check with the felt sense to see if the word or words really fit. Also there may be more than just a word needed, or more is there being ignored as they search only for words. I am very explicit here, saying, "Notice whatever is there that would describe the felt sense to you. Whether it might be that more words are needed, or that different words would fit more exactly, or other things are there in addition to the words. Things you might see, such as colors, body postures, motions, scenes, clouds, lots of space or very little, or things that you might feel, like is it warm or cool, hard or soft, in there."

At times the guide will notice that all the words are just telling a story, without there being a noticeable felt sense. Here it is important to remember to not get caught up in the story. For the focuser might be needed to be listened to so they can get to the felt sense, which can come at any point in the story and it would be important to stop in the middle to pay attention to the felt sense and not worry about their finishing the story. Or the guide might sense the story is a way to avoid going deeper at that time. Whatever the case, the guide can be listening for *how* the focuser is *in* the situation they are talking about. Then the guide can point to the place where something is there, a felt sense. I say, " That really touches something, or is there a deep place right there?"

This serves to help the Focuser know you are with them, and that you are noticing that there is a tender place. Here a helpful reminder of the attitude is good. I often say, "Be very gentle there, take your time, and see if it has enough space." Or at other times I say, "Is it alright to welcome the tears." My gentle tone indicates it is all right with me and we can be together keeping that place company.

So we are back to the start, the attitude that underlies all else. With more experienced focusers, they can tell you how they want you to be with them. Not needing to say as much perhaps, but always helping them to notice what you observe, and then checking to see if it feels right to their inner process.

ACKNOWLEDGMENTS

WE WOULD LIKE TO THANK all of the people who contributed to Bebe's book in various ways, including helping to transcribe print articles that did not yet exist in electronic form: Ina Bransome, Mary Elaine Kiener, Lyn Rosen, Carol J. Sutherland Nickerson, Leonard Grossman, Adrianne Nevon, Chiara Gelardin, Joke Van Hoeck, Jim Leonidas, and Jane Nelson. We also wish to thank Ann Weiser Cornell for her ongoing encouragement, for making available all of the original Focusing Connection issues, as well as for putting out the call for volunteers in her 19th Day Gazette.

This book could not have been completed without Leonard Grossman's ongoing assistance in carrying messages back and forth from Rosa to Bebe. We also greatly appreciate Estelle Carol's valuable improvements to the design of the front cover, and Sharon Schreiber's work soliciting reviews and stories about Bebe from her current and former students. Much gratitude to Ruth Hirsch for her skillful and sensitive editing work, and to Cheryl Luft for the lovely imagery of the cover photo.

IN CLOSING

For more about my approach to Focusing, please visit my website at www.FocusingForLife.org. You can also call me at 708-524-1114.

I would love to hear about your own experiences with Focusing, or how these insights have affected your own life.

CPSIA information can be obtained at www.ICGtesting.com
Printed in the USA
BVOW05s1902220115

384547BV00001B/6/P